How To Conquer
Arthritis

What the papers say about Vernon Coleman and his books:

'Perhaps the best known health writer for the general public in the world today' - The Therapist

'The man is a national treasure' - What Doctors Don't Tell You

'Vernon Coleman writes brilliant books' - The Good Book Guide

'The revered guru of medicine' - Nursing Times

'A literary genius' - HSL Newsletter

'He's the Lone Ranger, Robin Hood and the Equalizer rolled into one' - Glasgow Evening Times

'Britain's leading health care campaigner' - The Sun

'Britain's leading medical author' - The Daily Star

'Brilliant' - The People

'Dr Vernon Coleman is one of our most enlightened, trenchant and sensible dispensers of medical advice' - The Observer

'The patient's champion' - Birmingham Post

'The medical expert you can't ignore' - Sunday Independent

'The most influential medical writer in Britain. There can be little doubt that Vernon Coleman is the people's doctor' - Devon Life

'The doctor who dares to speak his mind' - Oxford Mail

'Man with a mission' - Morning News

'Dr Coleman is more illuminating than the proverbial lady with the lamp' - Company Magazine

'Refreshingly sensible' - Spectator

'Dr Coleman gains in stature with successive books' - Coventry Evening Telegraph

'He writes lucidly and wittily' - Good Housekeeping

'I admire your direct approach and philosophy in respect of general health, especially sexual health, environmental and animal issues' A.W.

'It's lovely to have someone who cares about people as you do. You tell us such a lot of things that we are afraid to ask our own doctors' K.C.

'I would like to thank you for telling us the truth' - R.K.

'I feel I must write and congratulate you ... your no-nonsense attitude, teamed with plain common sense makes a refreshing change. Please keep up the good work' - L.B.

'Thanks over and over again - good health always to you as you are fighting for a good cause in life - for the sick' - E.H.

'I only wish to God that we had a few such as your good self in Parliament, then maybe our standard of life would possibly be better' - H.H.

'I must admit that initially I thought that some of your ideas were extreme, but sadly I must concede that I was wrong' - C.D..

'I greatly admire your no nonsense approach to things and your acting as champion of the people' - L.A.

'I have now read and studied all your excellent books and have enjoyed and benefited from them immensely' - B.B.

'May I say that I think you have done a real service to all those who have the sense and patience to study your books' - B.A.

Other books by Vernon Coleman

The Medicine Men (1975)
Paper Doctors (1976)
Everything You Want To Know About Ageing (1976)
Stress Control (1978)
The Home Pharmacy (1980)
Aspirin or Ambulance (1980)
Face Values (1981)
Guilt (1982)
The Good Medicine Guide (1982)
Stress And Your Stomach (1983)
Bodypower (1983)
An A to Z Of Women's Problems (1984)
Bodysense (1984)
Taking Care Of Your Skin (1984)
A Guide to Child Health (1984)
Life Without Tranquillisers (1985)
Diabetes (1985)
Arthritis (1985)
Eczema and Dermatitis (1985)
The Story Of Medicine (1985, 1998)
Natural Pain Control (1986)
Mindpower (1986)
Addicts and Addictions (1986)
Dr Vernon Coleman's Guide To Alternative Medicine (1988)
Stress Management Techniques (1988)
Overcoming Stress (1988)
Know Yourself (1988)
The Health Scandal (1988)
The 20 Minute Health Check (1989)
Sex For Everyone (1989)
Mind Over Body (1989)
Eat Green Lose Weight (1990)
Why Animal Experiments Must Stop (1991)
The Drugs Myth (1992)
Why Doctors Do More Harm Than Good (1993)
Stress and Relaxation (1993)
Complete Guide to Sex (1993)
How to Conquer Backache (1993)

Betrayal of Trust (1994)
Know Your Drugs (1994, 1997)
Food for Thought (1994)
The Traditional Home Doctor (1994)
I Hope Your Penis Shrivels Up (1994)
People Watching (1995)
Relief from IBS (1995)
The Parent's Handbook (1995)
Oral Sex: Bad Taste And Hard To Swallow? (1995)
Why Is Pubic Hair Curly? (1995)
Men in Dresses (1996)
Power over Cancer (1996)
Crossdressing (1996)
How To Get The Best Out Of Prescription Drugs (1996)
How To Get The Best Out of Alternative Medicine (1996)
How To Conquer Arthritis (1996)
High Blood Pressure (1996)
How To Stop Your Doctor Killing You (1996)
How To Overcome Toxic Stress (1990,1996,2000)
Fighting For Animals (1996)
Alice & Other Friends (1996)
Dr Coleman's Fast Action Health Secrets (1997)
Dr Vernon Coleman's Guide to Vitamins and Minerals (1997)
Spiritpower (1997, 2000)
Other People's Problems (1998)
How To Publish Your Own Book (1999)
How To Relax and Overcome Stress (1999)
Animal Rights – Human Wrongs (1999)
Superbody (1999)
The 101 Sexiest, Craziest, Most Outrageous Agony
   Column Questions (and Answers) of All Time (1999)

reports

Prostate Trouble (2000)
Vitamins and Minerals (2000)
How to Campaign (2000)
Genetic Engineering (2000)
Osteoporosis (2000)
Vaccines (2000)
Alternative Medicine (2000)

novels

The Village Cricket Tour (1990)
The Man Who Inherited a Golf Course (1995)
The Bilbury Chronicles (1992)
Bilbury Grange (1993)
Mrs Caldicot's Cabbage War (1993)
Bilbury Revels (1994)
Deadline (1994)
Bilbury Country (1996)
Second Innings (1999)
Around the Wicket (2000)

short stories

Bilbury Pie (1995)

on cricket

Thomas Winsden's Cricketing Almanack (1983)
Diary Of A Cricket Lover (1984)

as Edward Vernon

Practice Makes Perfect (1977)
Practise What You Preach (1978)
Getting Into Practice (1979)
Aphrodisiacs – An Owner's Manual (1983)
Aphrodisiacs – An Owner's Manual (Turbo Edition) (1984
The Complete Guide To Life (1984)

as Marc Charbonnier

Tunnel (novel 1980)

with Dr Alan C Turin

No More Headaches (1981)

with Alice

Alice's Diary (1989)
Alice's Adventures (1992)

How To Conquer
Arthritis

Vernon Coleman

European Medical Journal

Published in 1996 by the European Medical Journal, Publishing House, Trinity Place, Barnstaple, Devon EX32 9HJ, England.

Publishing history: *How to Conquer Arthritis* was first published by Hamlyn in 1993.

Reprinted 1997, 1998 (twice), 1999 (twice), 2000 (twice)

ISBN: 1 898947 94 5

A catalogue record for this book is available from the British Library.

Printed and bound by: J.W. Arrowsmith Ltd., Bristol.

NOTE 1

This book is not intended as an alternative to personal, professional medical advice. The reader should consult a physician in all matters relating to health, and particularly in respect of any symptoms which may require diagnosis or medical attention.

While the advice and information in this book are believed to be accurate at the time of going to press, neither the author nor the publisher can accept any legal responsibility or liability for any errors or omission that may be made.

NOTE 2

You must consult your doctor before changing your diet or beginning any exercise programme.

CONTENTS

CHAPTER ONE
WHAT IS ARTHRITIS?

Introduction

The word 'arthritis' is often used as though it referred to a
single disease. But the word 'arthritis' is about as useful and as
specific as the word 'infection'. If your doctor tells you that
you have arthritis he is simply telling you that you have a disease in which your joints are inflamed.

Just as there over a hundred different types of infection
so there are over a hundred different types of arthritis which
differ enormously in the speed with which they develop, the
length of time they last and the amount of damage and crippling that they do. Rheumatoid arthritis and osteoarthritis are
both types of arthritis but they are as different to one another as
are malaria and tuberculosis - which are both types of infection. Arthritis is so common that most of us will suffer from at
least one sort of it at least once in our lives. And because most
varieties of arthritis are incurable once the disease has developed it often lasts for life.

Few diseases affect as many people as the diseases in the
arthritis group; few cause as much pain, discomfort and disablement and few are the subject of so many myths and so much
misunderstanding. The longer you live the more likely you are
to suffer from arthritis. It doesn't matter whether you have an
active life or a quiet life - whatever sort of life you lead there
will be a type of arthritis that will, sooner or later, affect you to
some degree or another.

That is, as they say, the 'bad news'.

The 'good news' is that although arthritic diseases are
usually incurable the symptoms can usually be controlled. Arthritic diseases do not usually kill and if treated with care and

respect it is usually possible to minimise the amount of damage that is done and to control the crippling and the pain.

Just a few years ago arthritis sufferers faced a lifetime of disablement and more or less constant pain. We still haven't found a 'cure' for arthritis - any more than we have found a 'cure' for infection - but we have acquired a good deal of information which should help you to stop your joints being destroyed, to relieve joint pain and stiffness, to restore lost joint function and to slow down - or even halt - the rate at which the arthritis spreads. Some arthritis treatments are, it is true, potentially hazardous. But many millions of patients around the world have been treated safely and effectively and have learned how to combat their disease.

Whether your arthritis has been caused by ageing, strain, wear and tear, an infection with a bacteria or a virus, an injury, a metabolic or a chemical abnormality, a hormonal abnormality or an immune system problem there will be things that you can do to protect yourself, to maintain your mobility and to keep your pain and stiffness to a minimum.

If the symptoms of arthritis are left untreated - or are treated half heartedly - then they will invariably get worse. The damage that is done may eventually be irreparable. But if, on the other hand, treatment is initiated early and with enthusiasm then the outlook can be greatly improved.

There are nearly two hundred different joints in an average human body. Your joints make it possible for you to move - to walk, run, skip and to wave your arms around - they absorb sudden shocks (such as when you jump up in the air and then land on a hard surface). Joints can repair themselves when they are injured or damaged and they can replenish their own supplies of synovial - or lubricating - fluid.

Each joint consists of two opposing bones and on the end of each bone there is a layer of white, smooth, gristle like material called cartilage which is covered with a capsule and kept moist with a special lubricating fluid. Tendons attached to the two opposing bones help to hold the joint in position.

Although your joints can protect themselves, and even repair themselves, there are times when things go wrong. Joints, like every other part of your body, can become diseased, injured or infected. Indeed, there are well over one hundred different joint diseases already identified and the chances are that there are quite a few more still unidentified.

The diseases which affect joints fall into six basic categories.

First, there are the inflammatory joint disorders in which the synovial membrane (which is responsible for producing the synovial fluid) becomes red, thick and swollen. The result is that the whole joint becomes red, painful and swollen - and also feels hot. If the disease is allowed to continue uncontrolled the joint will eventually be destroyed. The commonest disorder in this category is rheumatoid arthritis.

Second, there are the types of disease caused by 'wear and tear' in which the cartilage covering the end of the bones wears away, leaving bone rubbing on bone. In these diseases - known as 'degenerative' the joints involved gradually becomes stiff, painful and difficult to move. The commonest disorder in this category is undoubtedly osteoarthritis although the disease itself is ill-named for it is not, as its name suggests, an inflammatory disease at all. (The suffix -itis suggests an inflammatory disease, as in tonsillitis and appendicitis). Strictly speaking osteoarthritis should be called osteoarthrosis but to avoid confusion I will use the more common name throughout this book. Because it is usually caused by 'wear and tear' osteoarthritis is more common among elderly people.

Third, there is the type of arthritis in which the inflammation occurs not in or around the synovial membrane (as it does in rheumatoid arthritis) but in the area where the ligaments and tendons join the bones. Diseases where the ligaments or tendons are involved make up the third group of arthritis disorders and the best known serious disease in this category is probably ankylosing spondylitis which is, after rheumatoid arthritis and osteoarthritis, the third commonest type of arthritis. Disorders in this general category are usually known as 'periarticular'. Tennis elbow (in which the insertion of the tendon into the bone is damaged) and housemaid's knee (in which a bursa at the knee joint is damaged and swollen) are other diseases which fall within this group.

Fourth, there are some types of joint disease in which the problems are caused by the development of crystals within the joint. The best known disease in this category is undoubtedly gout - the well known pains associated with the disease are caused by the formation of uric acid crystals in the joint space.

Fifth, there are some types of arthritis known as 'infective'. In this category organisms such as bacteria or viruses get into the joints. The symptoms of infective arthritis can develop quite quickly and the pain can be extremely severe.

The sixth and final type of arthritic disease does not involve the bones or even the joints directly but the muscles which surround a joint. It is not, therefore, a true form of arthritis at all. When muscles are inflamed or strained the resulting symptoms can be very similar to arthritis of the joint itself. Many types of backache fall into this category. Fibrositis - also known as 'muscular rheumatism' - falls into this category and can affect several parts of the body at once.

How Your Joints Are Designed

Bones are the framework upon which the rest of your body is built. They have to be strong (bone is one of the toughest and most resilient materials known to man) and rigid. If your bones bent every time you put your weight on them you would collapse in an untidy heap every time you tried to walk. Your spine is the central part of your skeleton; your skull is balanced on top of it and your arms and legs are attached to it. Although they are immensely strong bones are made of living tissue -

they have a blood supply just like other parts of your body - and they can change their shape if your body is short of essential minerals such as calcium or if there is a constant need for extra strength in one particular area.

Joints are the junctions between bones and they too are essential for without them you would be unable to bend or to move around at all.

* The bones of your upper and lower leg give your legs basic strength but it is your hip, knee and ankle joints which enable you to walk, run, skip and hop.

* Your shoulder, elbow and wrist joints enable you to move your arms about.

* The small joints in your hand enable you to pick up and hold a pen, a paintbrush or a knife and fork.

* The joints between your skull and the top of your spine enable you to nod and shake your head and to turn it from side to side.

* The intervertebral joints within your spine enable you to bend your back.

Muscles which are attached to your bones produce movement by contracting (and then relaxing again) but it is your joints which make all movement possible. Without your joints your body would have the flexibility and mobility of a table. Without joints your arms and legs would simply be stuck stiffly to your sides of your trunk and your spine would be completely rigid. Your bones are, of course, quite solid. And if your joints simply consisted of the ends of two bones resting on one another every movement you made would be stiff, painful and noisy. When you ran the shock of hitting the ground would be transmitted up through every bone and joint in your body. The friction between the bones of your lower leg and the bones of your upper leg would be so great that every movement of your knee would be slow and difficult.

There are three types of joint in your body: synovial, fibrous and cartilaginous.

Synovial joints: In order to make your joints move more comfortably and to reduce the amount of friction between the bones in a joint the end of each bone is covered with a layer of cartilage; a tough, white, gristly substance which allows the bone ends to move smoothly on one another and which also acts as an effective shock absorber. There is less friction between two cartilaginous surfaces than there is between an ice skate and a skating rink! Unlike bone and muscle (both of which can repair themselves very well) cartilage wears out. It can also be damaged by accidental injury.

Around the outside of each joint there is a membrane - called the synovium - which regularly produces a small amount of a sticky substance called synovial fluid. This specially prepared fluid helps to keep the cartilage in good condition and also acts as a lubricating fluid. If the synovial membrane becomes inflamed it may start to produce too much synovial fluid or to produce synovial fluid of the wrong consistency.

Covering the membrane or synovium is the joint capsule which is thicker and tougher than the membrane and which is designed to seal and protect the joint. In larger joints which have to carry a lot of weight and are under a great deal of pressure (for example the knee joint) the capsule contains thicker fibres called ligaments which help to give the joint extra stability and to restrict and control the amount of movement.

The muscles which control the movement of your body are attached to your bones by tendons. The tendons are usually attached to the end of the bones so that they can get the maximum amount of leverage. Tendons are fairly easily damaged - particularly at the point where they are attached to bone because it is here that they are at their thinnest. Sudden or difficult movements can tear a tendon. When a tendon runs very close to a joint or bone and there is a danger of the two rubbing against one another there will probably be a small bursa - or fluid filled sac - to help reduce the amount of friction and to make movement easier. If a bursa becomes inflamed it may produce too much fluid and become swollen.

Fibrous joints: Not all joints need the full range of movement provided by a synovial membrane, synovial fluid and joint capsule. Sometimes a joint needs to be much stiffer and tougher. The joints between your teeth and the sockets in which your teeth rest, for example, do not need much in the way of movement but do need to be strong. Similarly, at the bottom end of the bones in your lower leg the joint between your tibia and fibula doesn't need any movement. That too is a fibrous joint. Fibrous joints allow no appreciable movement and the bones are fixed together by fibrous tissue.

Cartilaginous joints: These joints are a half way house between synovial joints and fibrous joints. They allow a small amount of movement but are very strong and are, compared to such joints as the knee, elbow and hip, immobile. The bones of your spine - the intervertebral bodies - are separated by intervertebral discs which act as shock absorbers. The amount of movement between two intervertebral bones is very small but when added together all the disc-bone joints give your spine a considerable amount of movement without losing much strength.

Your Knees and Elbows: Synovial Hinge Joints

Joints which only allow one main type of movement are called 'hinge joints' because they are like hinges! There may, in addition, be some rotational movement as well but this is not a property of the hinge joint itself. (See the elbow joint below).

Your knees
Each knee joint connects two of the strongest long bones in

your body - a femur and a tibia. Although the articular surfaces of these two bones do not fit particularly well together the ligaments and muscles around the knee are very strong and make the joint extremely stable. The patella is a small, triangular, flat shaped bone which sits inside the tendon belonging to the quadriceps muscle of the thigh and has two main functions: it minimises the amount of friction between the quadriceps tendon and the lower end of the femur and it provides the front of the knee with some protection from 'head on' injury. The patella is not particularly important and if it is damaged it can be removed without affecting the knee very much at all.

Your elbows
Each elbow joint connects the two bones of the forearm - the radius and the ulna - with the humerus, the bone of the upper arm. Your ability to turn your hand over (so that it is either palm upwards or palm downwards) is due to the existence of joints between the radius and the ulna bones.

Your Shoulders and Hips: Ball and Socket Joints

Joints which allow a wide range of movement are called 'ball and socket' joints because the end of one bone, which is shaped like a ball, fits into the end of the other.

Your shoulders
Your shoulders are the most mobile joints in your body. The head of the humerus is ball shaped and it fits into a cavity in the scapula bone. The cavity in the scapula is shallow and it is this shallowness which gives the elbow joint its exceptional mobility.

Your hips
The femur is similar in shape to the humerus - the bone of the upper arm - but it is bigger and stronger and the ball of bone on

its upper end has a neck - usually about two inches (5cm) long - which enables the ball to fit snugly inside the acetabulum (a deep cup-like cavity) of the hip bone.

Your Spine: A Series of Cartilaginous Joints

Your spine is strong enough to withstand pressures of several hundred pounds and is so flexible that it can be bent to form two thirds of a circle. However, the intricate system of muscles and tendons and ligaments which keep the whole thing together can easily be damaged or disrupted in all sorts of ways. The spine acts as a scaffolding for the whole of the body with the skull, ribs, pelvis and limbs all attached to it. Through its middle runs the extremely delicate spinal cord - so delicate that even a relatively slight physical abnormality can cause awful pains.

Your spine consists of 26 solid bones. It is these bones which give the back its strength. But if the spine only consisted of bone then you wouldn't be able to bend to tie up your shoe laces or to pick things up off the floor. So between the bones there are intervertebral discs which act as bendy shock absorbers.

In addition to giving your spine strength the vertebrae also provide essential protection for your spinal cord - your body's biggest nerve. The spinal cord carries impulses from the brain to the arms, legs and body and then carries messages back from those areas to keep the brain informed. Hundreds of individual nerves connect the spinal cord to the various parts of the human body. If your spinal cord is damaged then you will be paralysed -the precise nature of the paralysis depending on the place where your spinal cord is damaged.

The vertebrae
The top part of your spine - the neck region - consists of seven bones called the cervical vertebrae. Below them - making the

spinal framework for the chest - are the twelve bones which are called the thoracic vertebrae. Next, there are the five bones of the lower back - called the lumbar vertebrae. The sacrum (which, although it consists of five sacral vertebrae, is usually regarded as one bone since the five vertebrae are fixed or fused together) comes next and right at the bottom there are the four tiny vertebrae of the coccyx. Since these are usually joined together as well they are often regarded as one bone.

Altogether, then, the spine consists of a grand total of 33 bones. But because five of these bones are joined together to form the sacrum and another four are joined together to form the coccyx anatomists usually regard the spine as consisting of 26 bones. The bones at the top and the bottom of the spine - the cervical vertebrae and the bones of the coccyx - are the smallest. The largest bones in the spine are the ones which make up the sacrum and the bones of the lumbar region.

When people draw skeletons - with all the bones of the spine balanced one on top of the other - they usually draw the spine as being fairly straight. But it isn't. In fact, in order to help it cope with all the stresses and strains of normal every day life your spine has no less than four curves. Right at the very top of the spine the small bones of the neck (which are called the cervical vertebrae) curve forwards. Below this curve the thoracic vertebrae - the bones which make up the spine in the chest region - curve backwards. Next, there is the lumbar spine which curves forwards again. And finally, there are the sacrum and the coccyx which curve backwards.

The bones in your spine differ in size but despite that the bones do show a number of similarities. The back part of each vertebra, called the neural arch, is the most complicated part of each bone. There is a hole through the middle of each neural arch. The spinal cord runs through the holes in all the neural arches. There are several pieces of bone sticking out from the neural arch:

    * From the back of each neural arch spinous processes

stick out. These are the bony projections that you can feel if you touch your spine.

    * A bony projection called an 'inferior articular process' points down

    * A bony projection called a 'superior articular process' points up

    * From each side of every neural arch a 'transverse process' projects

    * There is a solid piece of bone called the 'body' at the front of each vertebra.

The spinal joints

Amazingly, the bones in the spine are joined together by a total of nearly one hundred and fifty joints. Every single one of these joints helps to hold the spinal bones together firmly to create the apparently 'solid' spine. These one hundred and fifty joints make your spine strong.

Arthritis can affect any of these joints and so the possibilities for pain and stiffness in the spine are clearly tremendous.

Every one of the 26 vertebrae which make up the spine is connected to the vertebrae above it and the vertebra below it. For example, consider the situation of the tenth thoracic vertebra. The bottom part of this vertebra - the inferior articular process - fits neatly and precisely onto the superior articular process of the vertebra below - in this case the eleventh thoracic vertebra. The top part of this vertebra - the superior articular process - fits just as neatly and just as precisely onto the inferior articular process of the vertebra above - in this case the ninth thoracic vertebra. At the very bottom of the spine the sacrum - made up of the sacral bones - is joined to the hip bones. At the top of the spine the skull rests on the first cervical vertebra. The thoracic vertebrae help to provide a solid foundation for the twelve ribs which protect the heart and lungs and form the foundation of the chest wall.

The disks between the bones

Unless your spine is really badly affected by arthritis it will still be bendable. And a perfectly healthy spine is amazing - it can be bent round in a quite remarkable way.

Clearly, if the spine consisted solely of bone this would be impossible. A solid spine - consisting of vertebrae fixed together - would not bend. It is the shape of the bones and the existence of the disks in between the bones which make the bending of the spine possible. The intervertebral disks which fit in between the individual vertebrae and which are known as the spine's shock absorbers help to make sure that your spine can bend and move in all sorts of different directions without a terrible crunching of bone on bone.

On the outside of each intervertebral disk there is a strong, fibrous case which is called the annular fibrosus. Inside that there is a soft very squashy interior called the nucleus pulposus. The nucleus pulposus is strengthened with fibre. The disks are particularly squashy because they are made up mainly of fluid - they have no blood and a very rudimentary nerve supply.

At night when you lie down in bed the intervertebral disks in your spine will expand and get larger as they fill up with food and with water. During the day, however, as you walk about, the vertebrae will compress the disks in between them and some of the fluid will be squeezed out. Because of this squeezing and compressing we tend to lose around half an inch (1.3cm) in height during the daytime. At night, when our disks can expand again, we regain our lost height.

Although the intervertebral disks play the most important part in giving the spine its movement the shape of the vertebrae themselves also has a part to play. For example, the first cervical vertebra allows your head to tilt sideways and to nod forwards and backwards; the second cervical vertebra (the one beneath it) allows your head to turn to the right and to the left and the other bones in the spine also allow you to move your spine a little.

Ligaments in the spine
The 150 joints which help to make up the spine are protected
and given added strength by the protection of a huge number of
ligaments; strong, fibrous and slightly elastic bands of tissue
which hold the two pieces of bone together wherever a joint is
formed. Because of the way the fibres which make up a ligament run the ligaments help to ensure that each joint is held
firmly and is able to move properly.

Can Joints Be Made More Flexible?

The range of movement in any particular joint depends upon
the shape of the bones, the design of the joint and the restrict-
ing actions of ligaments and muscles. You cannot do anything
much about the design of the joint (in other words you can't
turn a 'hinge' joint into a 'ball and socket' joint) and you can't
deliberately alter the shape of the bones in a particular joint
but, by training, you modify the restraining action of the ligaments and muscles which control the amount of movement in a
joint. Professional acrobats, gymnasts and dancers get a tremendous amount of flexibility in their joints but they usually
start their training very early in life and they always train hard
for long periods.

Why Are Some People Double Jointed?

Individuals who have an unusual amount of movement in a
joint are often described as 'double jointed'. 'Double joints'
are common in the joints of the hand. The implication is that
the extra amount of movement they get is due to the fact that
they have two joints or one unusually shaped joint. In fact,
none of this is true. People who seem to be double jointed are

usually merely able to dislocate a particular joint. There is usually an audible click as the joint dislocates. Occasionally, and more rarely, people who have an unusual amount of movement in a joint may suffer from exceptionally lax ligaments, abnormal ligament or muscle attachments or bony malformations.

Why Do Some Joints Make A Noise?

The clicking of joints can be caused by tendons or ligaments which slip, by joints dislocating or even by small bubbles of gas moving about. When a joint makes a grating noise it is usually because the cartilage has worn down and the underlying bones are rubbing on one another. Grating noises are usually painful but clicking noises are often completely painless.

CHAPTER TWO:
RHEUMATOID ARTHRITIS

Introduction

There is little doubt that rheumatoid arthritis is one of the commonest of all crippling, long term diseases. Although it usually affects the smaller joints - particularly those of the hands and wrists and feet - it can also affect the joints of the spine. However, when this happens the spine is usually the last part of the body to be affected and by then other joints will probably be affected. The neck is usually the first part of the spine to be involved. The initial symptoms of rheumatoid arthritis are usually pain, tenderness, swelling and stiffness of the joints that are affected. These symptoms, which can arrive quite suddenly or which may develop slowly over a lengthy period of time, are nearly always worst first thing in the morning. Many joints can be affected and sufferers who have rheumatoid arthritis badly may complain that their whole bodies are affected. The pain and aching is often also accompanied by a general feeling of tiredness, listlessness and of being run down. The symptoms of rheumatoid arthritis are unusual in that they may sometimes disappear almost completely without any warning - though, sadly, they usually come back again.

What Are The Causes of Rheumatoid Arthritis?

There is no known single cause of rheumatoid arthritis. Instead it seems likely that a number of different factors are responsible for its development.

1. Infection
It is possible that the development of the disease may be triggered by a virus (see auto-immune reaction below).

2. Inherited factors

Some genes transmitted from generation to generation seem to determine susceptibility to rheumatoid arthritis (i.e. whether or not you get it) while others determine the extent to which the disease develops (i.e. how badly you get it).

3. Food

It seems possible that certain types of food may make rheumatoid arthritis more likely. Meat - and meat products - may be a cause of rheumatoid arthritis. I will explain later on what sort of diet you should follow in order to reduce your chances of getting rheumatoid arthritis and in order to minimise your symptoms if you have already got rheumatoid arthritis.

4. Auto-immune reaction

Normally, your immune system helps to protect you against attack from infectious diseases. But because the changes which take place inside the joints when rheumatoid arthritis develops are similar to the changes which take part in other parts of the body when antibodies produced by the human body are fighting an infection many experts now believe that under some circumstances your body's immune system may be triggered to attack your joints - and in particular the lining of the joints - producing an inflammation of the synovial membrane which causes the well known symptoms of the disease. One of the blood tests commonly done to confirm the presence of rheumatoid arthritis in joints checks for a special protein in the blood stream. This special protein is an antibody - similar to the antibodies which your body produces when it overcomes an infection such as influenza or measles. No one really understands yet exactly how or why your body's immune defence system should attack the linings of your joints (it seems such a silly and pointless thing to do). But it may be nothing more complicated than a simple case of mistaken identity.

Normally, cells called macrophages wander around your body looking for foreign looking cells. If they find any they produce a chemical signal which calls for help. Within a short space of time the foreign looking cells will be surrounded by cells called 'killer lymphocytes' which grab foreign cells and either poison them to death or eat them alive. This is, in principle, how your body's immune defence system works.

Neither the macrophages nor the 'killer lymphocytes' are usually triggered into action by your body's own cells. However, if any of your body's own cells have become damaged and have lost their identifying marks then your 'killer lymphocytes' will deal with them just as effectively and as unsympathetically as they will deal with foreign viruses, bacteria or fungi.

In rheumatoid arthritis your macrophages and 'killer lymphocytes' may be triggered into action by the fact that certain cells in your body - notably the cells of the synovial membranes in your joints - have changed in some way. It is thought that this is where the virus may come into play for it is possible that a virus that you have picked up may change your synovial membrane in some slight way so that it looks 'foreign' to your macrophages and 'killer lymphocytes'.

Who Gets Rheumatoid Arthritis?

Rheumatoid arthritis is much commoner in women than in men. For every two men who get the disease there are usually four or five female sufferers. This difference may be due to some genetic factor carried on the female sex chromosomes. Rheumatoid arthritis also runs in families and if your parents, grandparents or brothers or sisters have or had rheumatoid arthritis then your chances of suffering from the disease are increased. Although the disease can start at any age it usually affects people between the ages of thirty and sixty, most commonly starting in early adulthood or early middle age. Rheumatoid arthritis has been found in countries all over the world and it affects members of all races but it is more common - and tends to be more severe - among the inhabitants of Northern Europe. No one really knows whether this is due to the climate, to genetic factors or to a localised infection.

How Common is Rheumatoid Arthritis?

It is difficult to say how common the disease is because not all sufferers seek medical help. Obviously, some patients have far more severe symptoms than others and they will nearly all visit their doctor for advice. However, patients with mild symptoms are likely to struggle on without visiting the doctor. Some will manage without any treatment at all while others will treat themselves or visit alternative medical practitioners. Severe rheumatoid arthritis probably affects about one in every two hundred people (with an even smaller percentage being affected so much that they become crippled) whereas mild rheumatoid arthritis probably affects about one in every fifty people.

What Happens To The Joints In Rheumatoid Arthritis?

The normal job of the synovium - the membrane which covers the joint - is to produce a constant supply of synovial fluid, the oily substance which lubricates, moistens and feeds the cartilage on the ends of the two opposing bones. It is the cartilages which take all the pressure when a joint is in action and it is the synovial fluid which ensures that the cartilages stay in good condition. When rheumatoid arthritis develops and the synovial membrane becomes inflamed the first thing that happens is that the membrane swells up as the blood vessels supplying it open up to bring more 'killer' blood cells into the area.

If you have an infected spot on your skin then the blood vessels supplying that area will open up in an attempt to take more white blood cells to the area to help tackle the infection. Your body's internal defence systems rely on your blood supply to get to trouble spots and when and wherever there is a problem the localised blood vessels open up to ensure that the local blood supply is increased to the absolute maximum. This is exactly what happens to the synovium in an inflamed joint that has rheumatoid arthritis. Your body assumes that there must be some external agent present (a bacteria, virus or some other foreign organism) causing the inflammation and so it sends teams of specialist 'killer' blood cells to the area to try to clear up the problem.

In addition to becoming swollen the synovium also starts to go red and to feel hot as the blood flow increases. Because the synovium gets its nourishment from its blood supply the increased flow means that it starts to over-produce synovial fluid and within a relatively short time the whole joint will become swollen with fluid and painful to touch or to move. Instead of making movement easier the extra synovial fluid makes movement more difficult than ever. Occasionally, particularly in the knee joint, the excess fluid inside the joint can build up such a high pressure that it bursts the joint capsule and escapes into the muscles of the calf.

The joint will by now be showing all the typical symptoms of rheumatoid arthritis: it will be swollen, it will feel hot to the touch, it will look red and it will be stiff and painful to move. Meanwhile, because the inflammation is still there, your body assumes that the underlying infection which it wrongly believes has caused the inflammation is simply proving too powerful and too resistant to the 'killer' cells in your blood supply. So your body responds by increasing the flow of blood still further - pumping ever increasing amounts of blood into the tissues and making things worse rather than better. All this means that the synovium just gets bigger and bigger and grows more and more, gradually spreading over more and more of the inside of the joint.

Eventually, the expanding synovium will start to damage the cartilage - the essential load bearing surface on the ends of the opposing bones of the joint. Instead of being nice and slip-

pery and making the joint move easily and smoothly the cartilage will become rough and pitted and will make movement
difficult and uncomfortable. In advanced rheumatoid arthritis
the joints which are affected will become deformed as well as
swollen and stiff. If the tendons and bursae which lie over the
joint are also affected by the inflammation then they will be
damaged in much the same sort of way and the area around
the joint will become tender to the touch and difficult to
move.

One of the tragedies of rheumatoid arthritis is undoubtedly the fact that the problems which develop are caused by the
body's own defence mechanisms mistakenly diagnosing a case
of mild inflammation as being caused by an underlying infection; overreacting and then pumping unwanted blood cells into
the area in such huge quantities that the joint becomes permanently diseased. It is, I suppose, rather like the fire brigade
turning out to a small fire and then causing far more damage
with their high pressure water hoses than has been caused by
the flames.

Normally, inflammation is a useful trigger. It encourages
your body's own defence mechanisms to act quickly and deci-
sively, limiting the amount of damage, getting rid of the cause
of the inflammation and encouraging the healing process. As
soon as it is clear that the underlying cause of the inflammation
has been dealt with your body will stop sending in 'killer' blood
cells. But in rheumatoid arthritis the inflammation doesn't go
away and it is your body's reaction rather than the inflammation itself that does most of the damage. The consequences can
be long lasting and, if untreated, permanently disabling.

Rheumatoid Arthritis Does Not Just Affect Your Joints

Rheumatoid arthritis is primarily a disease of the joints. It
causes stiffness, swelling, tenderness and pain in and around
the joints.

But if you are a sufferer it will not only be your joints which will be affected. Because the inflammation inside your joint (or joints) triggers an auto-immune reaction and inspires your body to send an increased blood supply into the joints which are involved the disease will affect your health in many other ways. Patients who suffer from rheumatoid arthritis often complain that they feel tired, easily exhausted, irritable and edgy. Most victims claim that they also have vague aches and pains in many different parts of their bodies. It is quite common for rheumatoid arthritis sufferers to complain that they constantly feel as though they have the 'flu. Many have night sweats and quite a few find that they lose weight (though this can be an advantage for as I will show later losing excess weight can help reduce the severity of the symptoms associated with arthritis).

Many people with rheumatoid arthritis show a slight rise in body temperature (partly because of the increased blood flow and partly because your body knows that one of the best ways to combat an infection - which it thinks you have) is by increasing your general body temperature. And because the blood system is concentrating on producing and disseminating 'killer' blood cells there may be a shortage of red cells - the sort which normally carry oxygen to the tissues. This shortage of red blood cells can lead to anaemia and to breathlessness and tiredness.

Finally, although it is usually the joints - and particularly the synovial membranes - which are affected by the inflammation associated with rheumatoid arthritis that same inflammation can sometimes affect other parts of the body. The skin, kidneys, eyes, nerves, heart, lungs and tendons can all be affected by inflammation occasionally and when this happens all sorts of other symptoms can develop. Bones may become thin and easily broken, lungs may be scarred and the skin may be ulcerated.

How Quickly Does Rheumatoid Arthritis Develop?

Very occasionally rheumatoid arthritis will start suddenly. It is possible for someone to go to bed feeling fit and perfectly healthy and to wake up the next morning with all the symptoms of rheumatoid arthritis in one or more joints. But it is much more common for the disease to develop slowly over a period of weeks or even months. The disease usually starts in the joints of either the hands or the feet. In a typical patient the joints of the fingers will become stiff and swollen and painful to move. Because it hurts to move the joints the patient will probably want to rest them as much as possible. And so the muscles will become weak and will start to shrink. The stiffness in joints which are affected by rheumatoid arthritis is usually worst first thing in the morning. Gradually, as the pain and stiffness in the small joints gets worse and worse so the generalised symptoms of tiredness and weakness will also develop.

Which Joints Are Affected?

Any joint in the body that contains a synovial membrane can develop rheumatoid arthritis. The small joints of the hands and feet are the ones most commonly affected to begin with. The joints in the middle of the fingers and at the bases of the fingers are probably the ones which are affected most frequently. Next, usually come the wrists and the knees. The ankles, elbows, shoulders and hips are affected less frequently.

Rheumatoid Arthritis Can Last A Long Time - But Usually Comes and Goes

The 'bad news' is that once rheumatoid arthritis has started to develop it will usually last for many years before burning itself out and ceasing to cause any more damage. The 'good news' is that the disease comes and goes and most sufferers notice that their symptoms quieten down after a year or two - although they may flare up occasionally. During an 'active' phase of the disease patients usually feel terrible in themselves and invariably wake up feeling stiff. Joints which are affected have to be loosened slowly and painfully and they often begin to get stiff and painful again in the late afternoon or early evening. Most sufferers who have 'active' rheumatoid arthritis have to do things slowly. Some patients have noticed that 'active' phases of their rheumatoid arthritis can be triggered by certain types of food or by doing too much. But others find it quite impossible to spot any factor as being responsible for a painful attack. During an 'active' phase the inflamed synovium usually does damage to the inside of the joint and so afterwards the amount of movement in the joint will probably be slightly reduced. The hands, which have small and apparently vulnerable joints, seem to suffer most and to show the most dramatic long term changes.

After a few years rheumatoid arthritis usually begins to settle down and the 'active' phases become less and less common. In some patients this 'settling down' occurs after just a year or two. In others it can take twenty or thirty years. Even if your arthritis has been 'active' for many, many years you should never give up hope that it will one day become 'inactive'. If your arthritis has been 'active' for many years your joints may have been permanently damaged and disfigured by the time it settles down.

The joints of the hands - which often look worst affected and which may be so badly damaged that fine movements are difficult or even impossible - are usually least painful in the chronic or non active stages of the disease. In contrast, the joints of the hips and knees - which have to carry a lot of weight - may not show a great deal of deformity but may be constantly painful.

Tendons Can Be Affected Too

Although rheumatoid arthritis is primarily a joint disease it can sometimes affect the tendons by which muscles are attached to the bones which make up a joint.Tendons are thin and rather cord like and when a muscle contracts the tendon is used to pull the bone into place. Inevitably, the pressure on and in the tendon can be very high.

Tendons can be affected in two ways.

First, tendons themselves may develop patches of inflammation. When this happens a lump or nodule may develop inside or on top of the tendon. Normally, tendons slide in and out of place quite smoothly and easily - often travelling through fairly close fitting tunnels so that they do not interfere with (or get troubled by) other tissues. But when a nodule develops on a tendon the tendon may have difficulty in sliding in and out of its tunnel. To begin with the tendon may move in and out of position with an audible 'click' but if the lump gets big enough the tendon will eventually start to stick in one position. For a while it may be possible to force the lumpy tendon through its tunnel but if the lump gets big enough the tendon will stick permanently in one position.

Second, because the narrow tissue tunnels through which many tendons pass are lined with exactly the same sort of synovial membrane as that which lines and lubricates the inside of the joint the inflammation of rheumatoid arthritis may cause the inside of the tunnel to become swollen. The result will be that the tunnel becomes narrower and stickier - and so, not surprisingly, the tendon will tend to stick in one position. If the tendon remains stuck in one position for long enough there is a real danger that the inflamed synovial membrane will start to 'eat' it in just the same way that the inflamed synovial membrane inside a joint will eat into the cartilage surfaces on the tops of the bones. Eventually, there is a danger that the tendon will become weak and may tear apart with the result that the muscle is no longer connected to the bone that it is supposed to move. Inevitably, the result is then a paralysis. Putting a joint in a splint can sometimes help encourage the torn tendon to heal itself and if that fails it is often possible to repair a tendon surgically - simply sewing together the two separated halves.

Joint Damage May Result In Disablement

Because of the damage done inside the joints that are affected patients with rheumatoid arthritis sometimes become disabled. If the hands are badly affected by damaged joints or displaced or torn tendons the fingers may bend to one side or individual fingers may bend in a variety of different directions making it difficult to use the hand. If the toes are badly affected then walking may be made difficult. Patients who have bad arthritis in their feet complain that walking - even in comfortable shoes -is like walking on a stony beach in bare feet. If the toes become displaced in the same way that fingers often are then the foot probably won't fit into a normal shoe. If the elbows are badly affected then the sufferer may have difficulty in bending or straightening his arm. This can make all sorts of things - from washing to eating to tooth cleaning - extremely difficult. If the knees or hips are badly deformed then walking can be difficult.

Warning

If you have painful arthritis in your knees that keeps you awake at night you may want to relieve your pain by putting a pillow under your knees. DON'T. If your knees stiffen in a bent position (as they may) you will be permanently stuck with bent knees - and you will find walking extremely difficult.

Rheumatoid Arthritis Can Cause Inactivity and Depression

Not surprisingly the constant pain and disablement caused by rheumatoid arthritis often cause depression. It would be a surprise if such a far reaching and devastating disease did not make many sufferers miserable. Patients with rheumatoid arthritis often find it difficult to get out and about. They find sports difficult to play and often it is easier to stay at home slumped in an easy chair than to go out with friends or pursuing hobbies. But staying slumped in a chair or in bed can produce problems itself. First, there are the physical hazards. Staying immobile for long periods can result in muscles become weaker than ever and in bones become thinner and more likely to break. Areas of skin which support the body can develop pressure sores. Sitting or lying down for long periods means that the body's need for food goes down - and since most people who spend long periods sitting or lying eat too much that means a dangerous and destructive weight gain. Infections are far more likely in people who don't move about and remain active and, of course, the joints are more likely to get so stuff that movement becomes quite impossible. Finally, people who spend a lot of time keeping still tend to become less tolerant of pain when it occurs. And thus a vicious circle develops. Second, there are the mental hazards. If you allow your rheumatoid arthritis to run your whole life you will quickly become demoralised and miserable. Boredom and anxiety and fear quickly lead to an increased susceptibility to stress and a far greater liability to depression.

What Tests Can Be Done For Rheumatoid Arthritis?

Because rheumatoid arthritis is common and because the symptoms are pretty obvious it isn't usually too difficult to make the diagnosis clinically - without any hospital or laboratory tests. But the diagnosis isn't always easy to make - particularly in the early stages of the disease.

* Blood tests may show the existence of a substance called 'the rheumatoid factor' and may show that there is inflammation in the body. Blood tests can usually provide useful results early on in the history of the disease.

* X rays may show that the edges of the bones are damaged. But X rays do not usually show up any noticeable abnormalities until the rheumatoid arthritis has been present for many months or even years.

* Testing the synovial fluid - taken out of the joint - may show the presence of the disease

Repeating tests may enable doctors to tell how fast the disease is progressing.

Can Rheumatoid Arthritis Be Treated?

Rheumatoid arthritis cannot be cured but it can be treated and it is much easier to prevent complications developing than it is to treat them once they have developed. Never forget that although rheumatoid arthritis can disable you it is extremely unlikely to kill you.

The Right Attitude Is Vital

If you approach your arthritis gloomily - anxious about possible disablement and depressed by the fact that there is no 'magic' cure available - then the disease will do you far more damage than if you approach the problem in a positive, even aggressive, frame of mind. Reading this book will help you enormously because the more you know about the disease the greater your chance of combatting it successfully. There are many things that your doctor can do to help you - and you must always talk to your doctor before starting or changing any treatment. But there are also many things that you can do to help yourself - and approaching your disease in a positive frame of mine is one of the most important.

What Can Doctors Do To Help Combat Rheumatoid Arthritis?

Drug therapy

There are scores of drugs available for the treatment of arthritis - in all its forms - and the number of drugs available is growing every month. Many patients with rheumatoid arthritis need to keep taking drugs for months or even years and that means that there are huge potential profits to be made by companies which can market safe and effective drugs. It is hardly surprising, therefore, that many drug companies produce at least one drug designed for the relief of the joint symptoms such as pain and stiffness which are commonly caused by rheumatoid arthritis.

Aspirin and Co: the non steroidal anti-inflammatory drugs

The 'non steroidal anti-inflammatory drugs' are the ones most. commonly prescribed and drugs in this category work in three different ways:

* They reduce inflammation
* They help conquer pain
* They reduce any fever that may be present

Selecting the right drug for the right patient is always something of a problem. Some patients will respond to one drug while others will respond best to another substance. It is often a question of trial and error before the right drug is found. Surprisingly, perhaps, the drug that is still most widely prescribed - and which still seems to offer the greatest number of patients the greatest amount of relief - is still aspirin; the first 'non steroidal anti-inflammatory drug'. Aspirin has an unfortunate reputation for causing stomach bleeding but when used properly and carefully and prescribed in the soluble form it is as safe as most of the competing products. During the last decade or so an enormous number of 'safe' alternatives have been produced and time and time again it has been shown that many of the 'newest' and 'latest' drugs may also produce similar symptoms if used in decent quantities or for fairly long periods. The main disadvantage with aspirin is that it needs to be taken fairly regularly and patients using it invariably have to take tablets every four hours or so. Some patients do develop allergies to aspirin and tinnitus (noises in the ears) and deafness can also be a problem occasionally.

Because aspirin is made by numerous different companies and sold at very competitive prices most drug companies prefer to manufacture and promote their own alternatives - which can be sold at a much higher price and which can, therefore, be far more profitable. There are, therefore, scores of alternatives available which have roughly similar properties. It is impossible to recommend any one of these drugs as being better than any other and new drugs are launched virtually every month. Although there are many chemical differences between the drugs which are available most work by relieving both pain and inflammation. Most doctors have their own favourite drugs with which they become familiar, though some doctors do tend to prescribe the latest (and probably the most expensive) product that the drug salesmen tell them about. The only advantage of the huge variety of 'non steroidal anti-inflammatory drugs' (known as NSAIDS) is that if you fail to get relief from one drug there will almost always be another drug for you to try.

Corticosteroids (also known as 'steroids')
Corticosteroids suppress inflammation so effectively that when they were first introduced they were hailed as 'miracle' drugs. They mimic the actions of corticosteroid hormones produced within the body as an internal anti-inflammatory. Unfortunately, although (or perhaps that should be 'because') they are very

powerful corticosteroids can cause very serious side effects. They can produce stomach troubles, blood pressure problems, bone disorders, skin diseases and a characteristic swelling of the face and body. There is also a danger that if you take a corticosteroid for too long your body's own production of steroids will shut down and you will become dependent on the tablets you are taking.

Getting The Best Out Of Medicines

Sadly, many doctors do not really understand exactly how drugs work and what they can and cannot do. However, if you are going to benefit properly from the drugs you are prescribed it is vitally important that you understand just how drugs work and what you can expect from them. One survey which was done recently showed that a majority of patients - and this includes patients who are at home and patients receiving in patient hospital attention - receive only one quarter of the dose of pain killer they need in order to provide them with proper relief!

This is not, of course, because doctors or nurses are mean spirited or uncaring.There are several reasons for the medical profession's failure to give patients enough pain killers.

First, it is very easy for both doctors and nurses to underestimate the amount of pain a patient is suffering. Lots of patients try to be brave and try not to show just how much pain they are in. Inevitably, therefore, when doctors prescribe pills they don't prescribe in large enough doses or quantities.

Second, both doctors and nurses worry a lot about their patients getting hooked on the drugs they are taking. They worry about this because some pain killers - and in particular the morphine derivatives - are addictive. In fact this fear is to a very large extent unfounded. It is very rare for patients to get hooked on pain killers - even if they need to take quite large doses for long periods of time. Indeed, the risk of addiction seems to be greater if a patient does not receive his drug often enough or in adequate quantities to control the pain. When a patient has to suffer pain and wait for his drug he is more likely to get hooked on that drug than when the dosage and the timing are designed to enable the patient to avoid pain or to control the pain properly.

One of the most important things you should remember is that you will suffer far less if you take your pain killers regularly according to the clock rather than waiting for the pain to return before taking them. If you only take your pain killer when your pain is terrible your body will be weakened and you will be learning to link your drug with relief from pain: that is what is likely to lead to drug dependence. My advice is that anyone taking a drug of any kind should talk to his or her doctor about the medication. Find out what the drug is prescribed for; find out whether the drug is likely to be needed as a long term measure or a short term measure and ask your doctor to explain to you how the drug does its job. If your doctor doesn't know the answers to these questions then maybe your questions will help to make sure that he does a little homework himself so that he can answer your questions and learn a little more himself.

What You Should Know About Drugs

1. *How many times a day should they be taken:* If a drug has to be taken once a day it doesn't usually matter at what time of day it is taken as long as it is taken at the same time of day. A drug that needs to be taken twice a day should usually be taken at intervals of twelve hours. And a drug that needs to be taken three times a day should usually be taken at eight hour intervals if you are going to get the best out of it.

2. *Does it matter whether the drug is taken before, during or*

after meals: Some drugs are not absorbed properly if taken with food - other drugs may cause stomach problems and need to be taken with meals.

3. *For how long must a drug be taken*: Some drugs need to be taken as a complete course - others can be stopped when symptoms cease. It is essential that you know which of the drugs you take fall into which of these categories.

4. *What side effects can you expect*: You should ask your doctor if there are any particular side effects that you should watch out for. And if you notice any side effects of symptoms while taking a drug you should get in touch with your doctor straight away, report what you have noticed and ask him whether you should keep on with the pills or whether you should stop them. Common side effects with pain relievers include constipation, indigestion, dizziness and nausea and vomiting. But it is important to remember that all drugs can cause side effects and that the range of possible side effects is virtually infinite.

Suppositories

When you swallow a tablet or a pill the active constituent in that pill gets into your bloodstream and therefore the rest of your body by being digested as it travels along the intestinal tract. As far as the drugs used to control arthritic symptoms are concerned the main danger with this method is that the walls of the stomach may be irritated by the drug. Gastritis is, indeed, the commonest side effect associated with many of the drugs which are widely used in the treatment of rheumatoid arthritis. However, drugs do not have to be given by mouth in order to be absorbed through the digestive system and into the blood stream. In some countries the other end of the intestinal tract - the rectum - is considered a far more sensible place from which to start the absorption process. A drug taken as a suppository will be absorbed into the body just as quickly as a drug taken in tablet form but there will be a much reduced chance of any intestinal irritation. Although there may be obvious difficulties for patients with severe rheumatoid arthritis (putting a suppository into your rectum may be tricky if you have deformed, arthritic hands) the advantages are considerable and many drugs are available in this form.

Injections

Drugs taken by mouth or in suppository form have to travel throughout the whole body in order to have an effect on painful and inflamed joints. It is often more efficient and more effective to put the drug directly into the joint concerned. This does not only mean that the joint gets the full benefit of the drug but it also means that the patient concerned may be spared side effects which may be associated with the drug when it is used generally. When joints are being injected it is obviously important that the person handling the needle knows exactly what he is doing. Misplaced or carelessly or improperly administered injections can do far more harm than good. Some general practitioners do inject straight into joints (these are known as intra-articular injections) but the majority of patients will usually be dealt with by some sort of specialist - usually either an orthopaedic surgeon or a rheumatologist. The shoulders, wrists, elbows and knees are the joints most commonly tackled in this way, although other joints (fingers, toes and hips, for example) can be dealt with by injection. The drug used for the injection is usually a corticosteroid. The risks associated with drugs in this group are much smaller when the drugs are injected directly into a joint than when they are taken by mouth and allowed to spread throughout the whole body.

Before giving an injection into a joint the doctor will usually clean the area with an antiseptic and then give a local anaesthetic to numb the skin and the tissues just under the skin. The doctor usually confirms that he has the needle in the right place - right inside the joint - by withdrawing some of the fluid through the needle before giving the injection. Improvement usually follows about three days after an injection and will last for several months. A steroid injection can be repeated two or three times a year if necessary. Since infection can develop after an intra-articular injection it is important to tell your doctor straight away if you develop any unusual symptoms (such as increased pain, swelling, redness or heat) after the injection.

If a joint is swollen with an accumulation of fluid it may be possible to reduce the amount of pain and swelling and stiffness by withdrawing some of the excess fluid from the joint before giving an injection.

Surgery
Although surgery is used fairly frequently in the treatment of osteoarthritis its use is relatively rare in the treatment of rheumatoid arthritis. Here, however, are some of the operations that are sometimes performed in the treatment of this disease:

* Synovectomy: If the joint lining or synovium is badly inflamed it may be possible to prevent damage to the joint by removing the inflamed synovium completely. This operation needs to be performed at an early stage in the progress of the disease - before too much damage has been done. Similarly, if the tunnels through which the tendons pass are affected by an inflamed synovium an operation to remove the damaged tunnel may prevent problems in the future. These operations are usually performed at an early stage to prevent severe disabling or crippling developing.

* Joint replacement: Joint replacement operations were originally devised for use on patients with osteoarthritis where large joints such as the hip are commonly affected. Large joint operations have been so successful (nine out of ten operations on patients who need hip replacements surgery are successful) that surgeons are now replacing knee, elbow, shoulder, ankle and finger joints.

* Nerve relief: If a nerve is trapped by inflamed or swol-

len tissues the numbness, continuous pain and 'pins and needles' that is produced can be excruciating. An operation to free
the nerve and remove the pressure can produce spectacularly
successful results.

Physiotherapy

A good physiotherapist will probably want to see you walk and
sit and move before he or she even begins to examine you. By
watching the way that you move the physiotherapist will be
able to tell a great deal about your arthritis, the state of your
joints and the extent of your pain.Then, when he has studied
your movements, he will want to examine you. Physiotherapists don't just use their hands to heal their patients - they also
use them to find out what is wrong. By moving your joints and
by feeling your muscles a physiotherapist will be able to measure the extent of the damage done by your arthritis and will be
able to work out how best he or she can help you.

In addition to watching their patients move and examin-
ing them with their hands many physiotherapists also like to
look at any X rays that may have been taken - or, at the very
least, to look at the X ray reports written by the radiologist. In
addition they will also want to look at any blood tests which
may have been done.

Once they have thoroughly researched the patient's condition physiotherapists can start with their treatment. Unlike
drugs, which are often designed to offer nothing more than
short term relief, physiotherapy is usually designed to provide
some form of long term improvement.The type of treatments
physiotherapists use varies a great deal of course but their rep-
ertoire of therapies include massage, manipulation and exercise.

The sort of manipulation techniques used by physiotherapists are rather similar to the ones which are used by
chiropractors and osteopaths. It is vitally important that joints
and bones which are damaged are never manipulated (and it is

especially important that a damaged spine is never manipulated in any way since if it were there would be a risk of causing permanent damage to the spinal cord). It is also unwise to allow anyone to manipulate an inflamed joint or a bone which is weakened (this means that many patients with arthritis will probably not be suitable candidates for manipulation). When the joints and bones are suitable for manipulation the operator will often be able to unlock joints that have become fixed simply by using his or her hands. When properly used manipulation can help to relieve joint stiffness and muscle spasm.

A professional masseur (or masseuse) will stroke, knead and stretch your skin and muscles in order to relax them and to help take the stress and strain out of your joints. A good massage will help to break up toughened tissues and may even be able to help improve a poor blood supply. You can, of course, have a massage from a friend but a professional masseur is likely to be able to help relieve pains and stiffness far more effectively. As with manipulation you should not allow anyone to massage you unless your doctor has given his or her approval.

Ultrasound

Because it shows up soft tissues which cannot be shown very well on X ray pictures doctors use ultrasound to help them make a diagnosis. Physiotherapists on the other hand use ultrasound, which consists of high frequency sound waves, as a treatment aid to help them to mend injured ligaments, joints and muscles. Ultrasound is believed to help in several ways: it speeds up the ordinary, natural healing process; it increases the blood flow in the area and it also reduces the amount of inflammation.

Short wave diathery

Like ultrasound a full course of short wave diathermy is likely to involve two or three sessions a week for several weeks. And like ultrasound those who use this technique, which uses high frequency electromagnetic waves which create heat within the tissues, claim that there are few, if any, significant side effects and that it is painless.

Physiotherapists use short wave diathermy because they claim that it can help to increase the flow of the blood, speed up the healing processes which normally and naturally help to repair the body and reduce any swelling which exists. The precise type of treatment they use will depend upon the tissues involved for different types of treatment affect tissues at different layers.

Interferential therapy
Unlike short wave diathermy and ultrasound some experts claim that interferential therapy, another form of electrical treatment, does little to help speed up long term recovery and is more likely to provide a short term solution to pain. Like short wave diathermy and ultrasound this type of therapy is usually given two or three times a week for several weeks.

Aids
Patients who are disabled by rheumatoid arthritis may be able to help themselves by using some or all of the aids or appliances described on pages at the back of this book.

Stress Can Make Your Arthritis Worse

Case History
Michael had been an arthritis suffer for eight years when he came to see me complaining that the aspirin he was taking wasn't helping his joints at all. I was surprised by this news for although he has quite severe rheumatoid arthritis Michael has usually managed to keep his pain in check with nothing more complicated than ordinary soluble aspirin - a drug which he feels comfortable with. He has learned over the years how many tablets a day he can take without suffering from side effects

such as dizziness and he knows from bitter experience that some of the much more expensive replacements for aspirin can produce side effects which can be just as troublesome and often far more unpredictable.

When I examined Michael I could understand why he was complaining. His joints were more swollen and inflamed than usual and there were clear signs that his arthritis had flared up rather badly. We talked for quite a while and I could tell that Michael was upset about something. Being well aware that stress and worry can make arthritis worse I asked him if he had been under any unusual amount of stress recently.

For a few moments I didn't think he was going to tell me what had been happening. Then he swallowed hard, coughed and started to tell me his story.

Michael ran a small, old-fashioned printing business with a partner whom I knew he had known since his school days. The firm printed personal notepaper, hand bills, leaflets and so on - nothing too ambitious. They had never made a lot of money but they had always made enough to live on reasonably comfortably. Because I had been to visit their children once or twice when they had measles and chicken pox I knew that Michael, his wife and their two children lived in a smart semi detached house on the outskirts of the town. I had never met Michael's partner, who wasn't a patient of mine, though I thought I remembered hearing that he had a flat in an old building down by the docks. His parents were, I knew, extremely wealthy and owned a large bakery on the other side of the town.

'My partner committed suicide four months ago,' said Michael suddenly. 'It was a terrible shock. We hadn't been particularly friendly for quite a few years - I don't know why, we just drifted apart - but it was obviously a shock nevertheless.'

He bit his lip and fiddled with his watch strap for a moment. I thought he was going to cry but Michael wasn't the sort of man who found crying in public easy to do and he made a real effort and held the tears back.

'I'd hardly got over that when I had another shock,' said Michael. 'Three weeks after Robert - that's my partner - died a man came to see me from a firm of solicitors. He was acting for a betting shop and he handed me a writ. I knew that Robert liked a bet but I had no idea just how far the addiction had gone and how much money he owed. The writ explained that Robert owed the betting shop a great deal of money and that because he and I were partners I was being held legally responsible for the debt.'

I was amazed at this. I hadn't been aware that partners are legally responsible for all of one another's debts. I made my surprise clear.

'You aren't any more surprised than I was,' said Michael, miserably. 'I just couldn't believe it.' He paused. 'But it was true enough.' He told me that he had been advised that he would have to sell the printing business and his home but warned that even then there probably would not be enough money to pay Robert's debts.

'The solicitor I went to see told me that I'll probably have to go into bankruptcy,' Michael told me. 'And as if all that wasn't enough my arthritis is now playing me up!' he said. 'I don't think it has ever been this bad.'

It was pretty clear to me just why Michael's arthritis had flared up. The exceptional stress he was under had almost certainly had a dramatic effect on his immune system with the result that the rheumatoid arthritis had reached an unprecedented peak of pain and discomfort.

With a heavy heart and little hope that it would help very much I prescribed a different anti inflammatory drug for Michael. I had little faith in the drug because I suspected that the stress Michael was under would continue to have a powerful and probably irreversible and uncontrollable influence on his body. I tried to hide my lack of faith because I am well aware that a doctor's enthusiasm for the remedy he is prescribing can have a powerful influence on its effectiveness.

I asked Michael to come back and see me again in two week's time but he didn't appear. When a month had passed and I still hadn't seen Michael again I called in at his home to see how he was.

He wasn't there but Judy, his wife, was.

'Michael meant to ring you and let you know what happened,' she told me. She seemed very happy for a woman who was about to be thrown out of her home. 'He didn't come back to see you again because his arthritis settled down just as suddenly as it had flared up. It's fine now. In fact Michael is out sailing today!'

I looked at her, surprised. 'I'm delighted! Did the pills help then?'

Michael's wife blushed. 'I'm afraid I don't think it was the pills,' she said. 'In fact I don't even think Michael started them. But two days after he had been to see you our solicitor rang us to say that Robert's parents had been so upset when they had heard about what had happened that they had paid the bookmaker themselves.'

'So Michael isn't responsible any more?'

Judy shook her head. 'We don't have to sell the house,' she said. 'And we don't even have to sell the printing firm. Robert's parents are going to keep Robert's share of the business but we don't have to sell it.' She looked at me and smiled. 'You probably won't believe the difference it made to Michael,' she said. 'One day he could hardly walk and he was in a lot of pain. The next day he was back to normal!'

But I did believe her.

Stress is one of the most powerful causes of arthritis. There isn't always a quick solution, as there was in Michael's case, but many arthritis victims could help themselves enormously if they learned how to reduce their exposure and increase their resistance to stress.

How to relax your body
When you are anxious, nervous or under stress in any way your mind deliberately tenses up the muscles around your body. There is a long established, sensible reason for this. By tensing up muscles your mind is preparing your body for action; it assumes that the best way to deal with the threat you are facing will be physical action. Your mind is getting your body ready to fight or to run away. But most modern stresses cannot be dealt with by a physical response. You cannot fight a traffic jam and running away from an electricity bill won't do you any good. Modern stresses persist for long periods - and so muscles remain tense for long periods too. Tensed muscles commonly produce headaches, backache and stiff necks. Eight out of ten cases of backache are caused by stress and a staggering 98% of headaches are produced in the same way.

Learning how to avoid unnecessary stresses, how to build up your resistance to stress and how to improve your ability to cope with stress will all help you combat muscle tension. But there is another, more direct way, to tackle muscle tension and the associated problems it produces: deliberately relaxing your tensed muscles.

Relax your body
Make sure that you will not be disturbed for at least twenty minutes then lie down somewhere quiet and comfortable and use this simple-to-learn technique to help relieve muscle tension.

1. Take very deep, slow breaths. Stress will make you breathe more quickly than usual so soothe your mind - and your body - by deliberately taking slower, deeper breaths.
2. Clench your left hand as tightly as you can, making a fist with your fingers. Do it well and you will see the knuckles go white. If you now let your fist unfold you will feel the muscles relax. When your hand was clenched the muscles were tensed;

unfolded the same muscles are relaxed. This is what you must do with the other muscle groups of your body.

3. Bend your left arm and try to make your left biceps muscle stand out as much as you can. Then relax it and let the muscles ease. When your arm is thoroughly relaxed let it lie loosely by your side.

4. Clench your right hand as tightly as you can, making a fist again with your fingers. When you let your fist unfold you will feel the muscles relax.

5. Now bend your right arm and make your right biceps muscle stand out as much as you can. Then relax it and let the muscles become relaxed. When your arm is thoroughly relaxed let it lie loosely by your side.

6. Tighten the muscles in your left foot. Curl your toes upwards. And then downwards. When your foot feels as tense as you can make it deliberately relax the muscles.

7. Tense the muscles of your left calf. You should be able to feel the muscles in the back of your left leg become firm and hard as you tense them. Bend your foot up towards you to help tighten the muscles. Then let the muscles relax.

8. Straighten your left leg and point your foot away from you. You will feel the muscles on the front of your left thigh tighten up - they should be firm right up to the top of your leg. Now relax those muscles and let your left leg lie loosely on the bed.

9. Tighten the muscles in your right foot. Curl your toes upwards. And then downwards. When your foot feels as tense as you can make it deliberately relax the muscles.

10. Tense the muscles of your right calf. You should be able to feel the muscles in the back of your right leg become firm and hard as you tense them. Bend your foot up towards you to help tighten the muscles. Then let the muscles relax.

11. Straighten your right leg and point your foot away from you. You will feel the muscles on the front of your right thigh tighten up - they should be firm right up to the top of your leg. Now relax those muscles and let your right leg lie loosely on

the bed.

12.Lift yourself up by tightening your buttock muscles. You should be able to lift your body upwards by an inch or so. Then let your muscles fall loose again.

13. Tense and contract your abdominal muscles. Try to pull your abdominal wall as far in as possible. Then let go and allow your waist to reach its maximum circumference.

14. Tighten up the muscles of your chest. Take a big, deep breath in and strain to hold it for as long as possible. Then, slowly, let it go.

15. Push your shoulders backwards as far as they will go, then bring them forwards and inwards. Finally, shrug them as high as you can. Keep your head perfectly still and try to touch your ears with your shoulders. It will probably be impossible but try anyway. Then let your shoulders relax and ease.

16. Next tighten up the muscles of your back. Try to make yourself as tall as you can. Then let the muscles relax.

17. The muscles of your neck are next. Gently, turn your head first one way and then the other. Then let the muscles of your neck relax. Move your head around and make sure that your neck muscles are completely loose and easy.

18. Move your eyebrows upwards and then pull them down as far as they will go. Do this several times, making sure that you can feel the muscles tightening both when you move your eyebrows up and when you pull them down. Then let them relax.

19. Screw up your eyes as tightly as you can. Pretend that someone is trying to force your eyes open. Keep them shut tightly. Then, keeping your eyelids closed, let them relax.

20. Move your lower jaw around. Grit your teeth. Wrinkle your nose. Smile as wide as you can showing as many teeth as you can. Push your tongue out as far as it will go, push it firmly against the bottom of your mouth and then the top of your mouth before letting it lie easy and relaxed inside your mouth. Now let all your facial muscles go loose and relaxed.

How to relax your mind

We tend to think of our imaginations as fairly insignificant, light hearted parts of our minds. That is a mistake that can prove deadly. The too often unrecognised truth is that the human imagination is powerful enough to kill. And the only person your imagination is likely to kill is you.

It is usually assumed that stress causes ill health because our bodies cannot cope with the strain of too much work, too much aggravation or too much excitement. But a good deal of the damage caused by stress is a consequence not of the real problems you may face but of the imaginary consequences your mind creates from those real problems; your imagination converts the often minor stresses of the present into major stresses of the future.

For example, when you get up in the morning and find an electricity bill waiting for you your immediate response will depend upon your ability to pay the bill. If you cannot pay the bill the next response will be for your imagination to swing into action and to create a scenario detailing what might happen as a result of your inability to pay. You may 'see' yourself being issued with a summons; being taken to court and publicly disgraced; being put in prison; losing your job; losing your home; losing your friends; being separated from your family and so on and so on. As you sit in your kitchen looking at the electricity bill none of these things are real. But once the electricity bill has triggered your imagination into action these imaginary consequences will have a very real effect on your body. As you become increasingly worried and apprehensive so your blood pressure will rise, your muscles will become tense and acid will pour into your stomach to prepare your body for immediate action. In a very short time your imagination will have triggered an entirely inappropriate physical response. The result will probably be that within a few minutes you will end up with a headache or an attack of indigestion. It will not have been the electricity bill which will have done the damage but

your response to the arrival of the electricity bill; your headache won't be due to the piece of paper in your hand but to
your imagination.

And the same sort of thing happens all the time.

When you miss your train your imagination tells you that
you may lose your job and that if you lose your job you will be
unable to pay back the bank loan on your home. Standing there
on the platform your body responds not to the disappearing
train but to the loss of your home.

Have you ever watched a horror film on the television
and felt the hairs on the back of your neck stand up? If the film
was both frightening and convincing then, by the time it finished, you would have probably been scared enough to go
around the house checking the doors and windows - to make
sure that no intruders could get in!

Have you ever watched a film in which there were long
desert scenes? If you have then you've probably noticed that
by the end of the film you felt thirsty. When that happened
your body was responding to your imagination.

If you get an urgent message to ring someone close to
you your first reaction will probably be to worry. Your imagination will create a whole range of possible reasons for the
telephone call. Maybe, you will think, there has been an acci-
dent. Perhaps someone has died. If you cannot get through on
the telephone your mind will work overtime. Your imagination
will create an endless series of possibilities. At the very least
you will imagine a domestic crisis: a burst pipe or a fire in the
kitchen. At the worst - well, at the worst your imagination will
create a scenarios far more horrendous than life could create.
Your head will begin to ache, your muscles will tingle with
tension and you will probably feel nauseated and shivery with
apprehension. When you eventually get through and speak to
the caller and discover that they wanted to tell you that you had
won a small amount of money on a lottery your relief will be
instant.

And yet all the terrible things that have worried you half to death only ever existed in your imagination. Your mind creates major stresses out of minor ones because your imagination creates a horrific scenario out of every small incident. It is hardly surprising that the vast majority of illnesses are caused or made worse by stress. It is hardly surprising that the pains and disablement of arthritis are often caused or made worse by the stress of twentieth century life. That is the downside. That is the way that your imagination can harm your health. It isn't difficult to see that your imagination is an extremely powerful weapon; powerful enough to ruin your life or even to kill you.

But if you know how to do it you can harness the power of your imagination and use it to your advantage. Your imagination can create a major illness out of a series of minor anxieties. But, if controlled properly, your imagination can also help you to reduce your susceptibility to stress and to increase your ability to resist the potentially damaging consequences of stress laden incidents.

In just the same way that your imagination can make you ill so it can also make you well again. In the same way that it can exacerbate an existing illness so it can also help to protect you. All you have to do is to learn how - and that is no more difficult than learning how to swim or to ride a bicycle. Your body will respond to positive, hopeful, optimistic and peaceful mental scenes just as well as it will respond to dangerous, frightening or pessimistic images. So, in order to take advantage of the healing powers of your imagination you must simply learn to fill your mind with peaceful and relaxing images.

Relax your mind with a daydream
Imagine. It is a warm, sunny day in early summer. There isn't a cloud a the sky and there is a soft, gentle, delicate breeze in the air which stops the heat from burning and the day from being oppressive. It is a perfect day and for a few minutes you can forget all your fears, anxieties and worries. You are on a private

island; alone, content and away from all everyday pressures and stresses; safe for now from the one thousand and one demands which normally make life difficult and which sometimes make it unbearable. You are alone but not lonely. Around you the world is quiet but the silence is soothing. Occasionally, the breeze rustles the leaves in the nearby trees and in the distance you can hear insects in the grass, birds in the trees and the sound of the sea splashing onto the shore.

You are walking, slowly and effortlessly along a narrow country track. There are no cars, no people, no noises, no fumes and no rubbish on your island. You can take your time. You have all the time in the world. On your left there is a hedgerow. On your right a lush, green meadow. At the base of the hedge there are primroses. In the meadow early poppies are already unfolding their pink-red petals and dancing lightly in the whispering breeze. You are at peace with yourself and with the world in this private and lovely place.

You walk on knowing that no one will ever find you or disturb you here. This is your personal world. No one else can come onto your island without your permission. No one can interrupt you or threaten you or make you sad while you are here. You know that whatever happens elsewhere you are safe here.

Slowly, your track begins to curve around to the left. There is a slight incline too and you realise that you are heading down towards the sea. Your island is a small one and you can see the sea all around you. It is a deep, beautiful blue and it stretches away, unspoilt and unmarked as far as you can see. As you head down the track you gradually become aware of the fact that you can hear a stream nearby. You stop for a moment, move slightly to your left, and look through the hedge so that you can see the stream. It is quite shallow but the water runs fast and is sparkling and crystal clear. The bed of the stream is made of small, pretty looking stones though a few larger rocks poke up above the surface of the water.

Further down and closer to the seashore the stream spreads out and becomes even shallower. Standing on the far side of the stream there are a dozen sturdy but old and gnarled trees. Beneath them, in the shade, there is a soft, inviting looking, mossy bank. You stand for a few more moments and stare at what seems to you to be the most beautiful and peaceful spot in the world. If you turn to your left you can see the stream, meandering down the gently sloping hill-side of your island. If you turn to your right you can see where the stream trickles down, between rocks and across a stretch of soft, golden sand, to the sea.

Using half a dozen large, stepping stones you cross the stream, sit down on the mossy bank and rest your back against a tree. It is like sitting in the most comfortable armchair ever designed. There is nowhere in the world quite so beautiful as your island and there is nowhere quite so peaceful as this spot where your island stream runs down into the sea. You rest, alone, content and silent. You feel comfortable, rested and happy. When you close your eyes you can hear the clear water of the stream gurgling and bubbling over its rocky bed. In the distance you can hear the sea crashing rhythmically and majestically onto the rocks. Above you the breeze is rustling the leaves of the tree you are leaning up against. You can feel the warmth of the sun filtering down through the leaves and your whole body feels relaxed. You love this peaceful spot. You can stay here as long as you like. It is your island, your hideaway, your private escape from the real world. Here you can rest, untroubled by anxieties, stresses, pressures and worries.

And what makes this private place so very special is the fact that you can take it with you wherever you go. Your personal island will always be ready for you; will always welcome you and will always offer you peace and tranquillity. It never goes dark here. The sun never sets. It never goes cold. It never rains. This is your Camelot. This is your passport to peace, contentment and happiness.

Build up your self-confidence

Psychologists have known for years that arthritis sufferers tend to treat themselves harshly; they are often shy and dissatisfied with their own work; pushing themselves far too hard and constantly searching for a contentment and sense of personal satisfaction which escapes them. Arthritis sufferers often feel inferior and helpless to change their own destiny. Here is a case history from my files which illustrates how one arthritis sufferer benefited by learning to build up her self-confidence.

Case history

When Linda first came to see me she was in a terrible state. She had a bad skin rash on the backs of both of her hands and her asthma, from which she had suffered for most of her life, was almost out of control. She couldn't sleep and she was, she readily confessed, edgy and tearful all the time. Her long standing arthritis was crippling her so badly that she found it painful to walk.

'I just can't cope,' she told me, with tears forming in her eyes. 'I've got so much to do.'

I asked her to tell me exactly what she had to do and why she couldn't cope. When she had finished explaining things to me I wasn't surprised that she was in a complete state. I don't think anyone could have coped with the workload she had acquired for herself.

At the school where she worked as a teacher Linda had taken on the responsibility of organising the school play and of making all the arrangements for the summer fete. At the church she attended she had also been given the responsibility for organising the fete. And she had recently taken on the job as honorary secretary of the local tennis club. On top of all this she was trying to look after her aged and incontinent mother, her husband and her two teenage children. And to work full time as a teacher of art.

'I feel so incompetent,' she sobbed. 'I know I ought to be

able to do better but I just don't seem able to cope any more!'

'I'm not surprised!' I told her. 'You're trying to do far too much. How on earth did you allow yourself to be lumbered with so many jobs!'

Linda looked at me in some surprise and thought for a moment or two. 'I suppose its because I don't like to say 'no',' she confessed. 'I've never really thought about it before.'

And that was the key to Linda's problems.

She didn't like to say 'no'.

In fact, it was worse than that.

She couldn't say 'no'.

'Why do you think you can't say 'no'?' I asked her.

Linda thought for a long time before answering that question. 'I suppose its because I don't like to let people down,' she replied. 'I want to feel that I'm being useful. And if I even think of saying 'no' I always feel terribly guilty and end up saying 'yes'.'

After I had talked to Linda for a while I began to understand what forces were driving her to such a point of self destruction. (The arthritis, the skin rash, the asthma, the sleeplessness and the tearfulness were, of course, all a result of the stress Linda was under as a result of her apparently total inability to say 'no').

As a child Linda's parents had been very ambitious for her. They had pushed her constantly and had never really been satisfied with her school work. Not once, Linda told me with tears streaming down her cheeks, had her parents ever praised her. She couldn't ever remember anyone saying 'well done' or 'thank you' or 'that was kind of you'.

Linda had grown up desperately pushing herself harder and harder in a constant effort to please her unpleasable parents. When she had started work her total lack of self assurance and self-confidence and her constant search for appreciation and approval meant that she took on all the jobs that no one else wanted to take on. She quickly acquired a reputation as an over willing work horse. And when she married the same thing happened again. Her husband, and then her children, learnt to be lazy and to let her do everything for them. She did all the shopping, all the cleaning, all the washing, all the ironing, all the cooking and all the washing up. She even did the gardening!

And driving her on all the time was her burning need for approval from others. Everything she did was inspired by her deep rooted feeling of unworthiness and incompetence.

I explained to Linda that the only long term solution was for her to acquire more self esteem and self-confidence.

'Only by building up your sense of self assurance and by learning that you have rights as well as responsibilities will you be able to escape from the treadmill you're on,' I told her.

Over the next few weeks I tried to show Linda how she could do just this. To begin with I gave her a list of words to look at and I asked her to pick out any of the words which she thought applied to her.

Here is the list:

* Attentive
* Agreeable
* Ambitious
* Brave
* Chivalrous
* Conscientious
* Careful
* Creative
* Decent
* Decent
* Faithful
* Loyal
* Kind
* Intelligent
* Polite

* Punctilious
* Scrupulous
* Honest
* Truthful
* Respectable
* Unselfish
* Obedient
* Benevolent
* Impeccable
* Hard working
* Thoughtful
* Wise

'Oh I don't think any of those apply to me,' said Linda.

'Of course they do!' I insisted. 'You're certainly unselfish aren't you! And you're respectable surely?'

'Yes, I suppose so.' She paused and nodded. 'I suppose I am,' she agreed.

'And you are truthful, polite and benevolent?'

Linda agreed, after hesitating, that these words did accurately describe her.

'And you're attentive and agreeable and conscientious and careful?'

Again Linda thought carefully.

And then, when she had thought about it, again she nodded.

Gradually, I managed to convince her that she did have many excellent qualities. Indeed, by the time we had finished going through the list Linda had to agree that most of the words applied to her.

'But none of that makes me a good person,' said Linda. 'I'm always getting things wrong. I always seem to be making mistakes. And I just don't seem to be able to cope.'

'What sort of things do you get wrong? In what way don't you think you can cope?'

'Well, I bought the wrong sort of tea for my mother the

other day. And my daughter went mad at me because I didn't have her jeans ironed in time for her to go out on Saturday.' She stopped and looked down at her lap. 'I always seem to have to be apologising,' she said sadly. She shrugged. 'It happens all the time.'

'How old is your daughter?' I asked her.

'Fifteen.'

'Is she handicapped?'

Linda looked up at me. 'No.'

'Why didn't she iron her jeans herself?'

Linda looked puzzled at this; she had clearly never even thought of asking her daughter to help with the ironing.

'Why does it always have to be you who does everything?' I asked her. 'You are making yourself ill by trying so hard to do things for other people.' I explained to Linda that no one can do everything and that there is, in any case, no shame in making mistakes or getting things wrong occasionally.

'You need to be more selfish,' I told her. 'How much time in the week do you have to do things that you want to do?'

Linda looked at me as if I was mad. 'What do you mean?'

'When did you last do something for you,' I explained. 'Something that no one else wanted you to do.'

Linda frowned. She couldn't think of anything.

'You let people push you around and organise your life for you because you are constantly searching for approval and because you've got absolutely no self respect or self assurance,' I explained. 'And because you are trying to do the impossible your health is beginning to suffer.' I explained to her that disorders such as arthritis, asthma and eczema often attack individuals who are self effacing and who allow themselves to be pushed around by others.

'And you must learn not to worry too much about occasional mistakes,' I told her. 'It's impossible for anyone to be right all the time and there is absolutely nothing at all wrong or shaming about having to say 'I was wrong' or 'I made a mistake' occasionally. The only people who never have to say they were wrong are the people who never do anything, who never try anything and who, therefore, never take any risks.'

Slowly, Linda began to realise that she was not a bad person but that she was a weak person and that she was being pushed around at school, at home and everywhere else by other people who were taking advantage of her fears, her need for approval and her lack of self-confidence.

Gradually, I managed to get Linda to realise that she had many wonderful qualities; that she was kind and thoughtful and generous. I managed to persuade her to begin to think about herself a little more often; to take charge of at least part of her own life and to say 'no' occasionally to people who wanted her to do things for them.

Eventually, Linda came into the surgery one Saturday with a broad smile on her face.

'What happened?' I asked her.

'My daughter brought some friends home today,' said Linda. And when she found that I hadn't had time to do the washing up after breakfast she came storming in to complain.

'What did you do?' I asked her.

'I told her that I was busy and that if she wanted clean cups she could wash some up herself!' said Linda, looking both slightly pleased with herself and slightly embarrassed by her own cheek. I couldn't help noticing that her skin rash had cleared up.

'What did she do?'

'She washed up some cups!' said Linda, unable to contain her delight.

Linda will probably never be completely free of her ingrained desire to please other people. But she has, at least, made a start.

And when she left the surgery that day and I asked her how her arthritis was she turned and looked at me as though she didn't know what I was talking about.

'What arthritis?' she asked, with a smile.

It was a wonderful moment.

How to harness your positive emotions and conquer your negative ones

However careful you are to organise your life so that your exposure to unnecessary stress is kept to a minimum, and however skilled you are at maximising your ability to withstand stress and cope with pressure, there will always be moments when stress overwhelms your defences.

At those moments your natural tendency will probably be to respond not in any sensible, logical, analytical way but to respond instinctively and emotionally. Depending on the nature of the stress (and the way you feel about it) you may want to cry, shout, laugh or be plunged into deep despair. But in practice things are not quite this straightforward and natural responses aren't always the responses other people see.

Superficially your emotional responses may seem automatic and quite beyond voluntary control and you may think that when stress makes you sad you will cry and when anxieties make you angry you will shout but the relationship between stress and your emotions isn't that simple. Often your emotional responses to any given situation will be governed either by behavioural patterns which you learned many years before from parents, teachers and friends or as a result of prejudices acquired from people in authority or from people you respected. As a result you will subconsciously allow each natural, healthy response to be dominated and controlled by an intellectual response. Instead of crying you may stiffen your upper lip. Instead of shouting you may simply turn away and nurse your anger inside you.

Although this intellectual over-ride may have a certain social value (preventing you from making a fool of yourself in public) it will do your health no good at all and it will dramatically increases the chances of stress eventually having a devastating effect on your physical and mental well being. The contrary truth is that the more you learn how to give full reign to your emotions - whether they are positive ones or negative ones -the better you will be able to protect yourself against stress related damage and the happier and healthier you will be.

As I have already explained the vast majority of all the illnesses from which we suffer these days are caused by stress and all illnesses are made worse by stress. Our minds are killing us and making us pretty ill as they do it. Worry, anxiety, stress and pressure can cause an enormous amount of agony and real pain. But the opposite is also true. Just as negative thinking, unhappy thoughts and genuine problems can all make us ill so, in a similar way, positive thinking, happy thoughts, love, companionship and support can all help to keep us healthy and help us to get better when we are ill.

If you stop and think about it all this makes good sense. After all, if your mind can make you ill then surely it is only fair that it should also be able to make you well again.

Over the last few years some remarkable pieces of scientific work have been done by doctors keen to investigate the ways in which a positive approach can help to heal real illness. For example, consider this simple experiment which a doctor performed with 200 of his patients all of whom had symptoms but none of whom had definable illnesses.

The doctor divided the patients into two main groups. The patients in the first group were treated politely but were not given any firm assurance about when they would get better. The patients in the second group were told confidently that they would be better in a few days time.

When the doctor next saw his patients he noticed a remarkable difference between the two groups. Nearly two thirds of the patients who had been given positive encouragement had got better whereas only just over a third of the patients who had been given no encouragement had recovered.

This simple piece of research shows quite conclusively

just how significantly a positive approach can change our lives. Positive thinking can help to keep you healthy and it can help to minimise the length of time that your illness lasts. The inescapable truth is that you cannot escape from your emotions. Your emotions decide whether or not you are going to be happy, how successful you are going to be and how healthy you are going to be - by harnessing and taking advantage of your positive emotions and by conquering negative ones you can dramatically improve your health and your life expectation.

Don't be afraid to cry

I firmly believe that one of the main reasons why Italian men suffer less from heart disease than do British men (despite the fact that many of them eat the wrong foods, are overweight, drink too much and smoke too much) is that the former aren't afraid to cry.

British boys are taught that it is unmanly to cry. At school and at home they learn that crying is a girlish, wimpy thing to do. They are taught that they must respond to sadness, sorrow and despair with a firm upper lip; they are taught to 'bottle up' their natural emotions and to pretend that everything is all right. The boy or man who does cry will suffer twice: first, he will suffer the original pain and then he will suffer from a sense of guilt and shame for having cried.

Countless male leaders in Britain, America and Australia have lost credibility and respect through having cried in public. And yet crying is an important and effective way of dealing with stress; it is one of the body's most important ways of dealing with problems and pressures and it is, above all, an absolutely natural way of dealing with sadness.

When a baby cries it is making it clear to its parents that it desperately wants love and attention. When a child falls over in the garden and runs in crying to its mother it is making it clear that it wants reassurance and comfort. A mother who sees her child crying will pick it up, cuddle it, give it affection and show that she cares. The tears will attract sympathy and support when it is most needed.

The man who refuses to cry because he believes that it is a sign of weakness is putting himself at risk. By hiding his emotions he will turn a short term sadness into a long term frustration and turn a temporary despair into a permanent depression. Men who never cry are far more likely to suffer from stress related disorders as heart disease, high blood pressure, stomach ulcers and arthritis as are men who allow the tears to flow when they feel sad. It is now well known that people who suffer from arthritis are quite likely to have difficulty in expressing their emotions.

The man who hides his tears and turns his sadness inwards is storing up trouble for the future; by crying, and allowing his sadness to show, he would attract the love and the sympathy that can heal sadness; by refusing to cry he is making himself ever more vulnerable to unhappiness and ensuring that he will become yet another stress victim.

In recent years scientists have managed to confirm that crying is good for us. We know now that as well as attracting love and sympathy crying helps by getting rid of potentially dangerous chemical waste products which will otherwise build up in the body and lead to the development of depression.

When you cry because you are sad your tears are different to the tears you shed when you cry because you have something in your eye. The tears which are triggered by sadness have a different physical content to the tears which are inspired by specks of dust or gusts of wind.

Everyone should learn to cry when they feel sad; crying is nothing to be ashamed of - it is, rather, a natural and healthy response which invariably leads to a sense of contentment and a calmness which would otherwise be unattainable.

Deal positively with your anger
People who suffer from arthritis often have difficulty in show-

ing their anger. They feel bad about letting other people know how they feel and so they hide their angry feelings deep inside their souls. In the end, of course, that anger will show itself in some way or other - often by doing permanent damage to the joints.

Arthritis sufferers frequently feel that if they show their anger they will be exhibiting some weakness. The truth, of course, is very different. The truth is that we all feel angry occasionally. Even the most placid and peaceful person sometimes feels cross about some injustice or driven to anger by some series of frustrations. And the healthiest solution is often to show that anger - to let it out. If you hold your anger inside you, and refuse to let it out, then in the end it is you that it will damage.

Of course, I do not recommend letting your anger out in an unsociable or illegal fashion - that would merely lead to more frustrations and more injustices and more sadness and more anger! But there are lots of quite practical ways in which it is possible to get rid of accumulated anger in a healthy and useful way.

For example, you may be to get rid of your anger by performing some exhausting physical task. Maybe, if your doctor gives his approval, you have a garden you can dig (though it you do, then please be careful not to do too much too quickly - every year thousands of men and women injure their joints and give themselves backache by being too enthusiastic in the garden) or maybe you can give the house a spring clean.

Many people get rid of their anger through exercise. Maybe, if your doctor gives his approval, you could go to the gym and work out, or attend an aerobics class, or go for a run, or play a game of squash, tennis or football.

Whatever you choose to do you should, of course, remember that you must not allow your anger to make you forget all the safety precautions you have learnt. If you allow your anger to push you too hard then you will find it all too easy to damage a joint or to injure yourself - or someone else - in some way. You must consult you doctor - and obtain his permission-before you start any exercise programme.

Laughter can make you better

You may find it difficult to believe but there is now plenty of evidence to show that laughter can help overcome arthritis.

For example, consider the case of Peter. Peter had been a patient of mine for years and he suffered from terrible arthritis which made it difficult for him to move about. His spine, his arms and his legs were all affected to some degree or another. Over the years Peter had tried many different treatments for his arthritis - some of them orthodox and some of them from the 'alternative' range of therapies. But, sadly, none of the treatments he had tried had worked very well.

Even before he had contracted arthritis Peter had been a rather unhappy man. Some people are just rather doleful by nature; they find it difficult to enjoy themselves; they are full of responsibility even as children and when they grow up to adulthood they find their shoulders laden with troubles and worries. Peter was like that. He didn't laugh much before his body developed arthritis.

For several years I had never seen Peter smile. He worked as an accountant and he took his work very seriously. He didn't like practical jokes, he didn't like seeing people wasting time laughing and, to be honest, he didn't seem to have a very well developed sense of humour.

I talked to him about this one day. I explained to him that an American writer called Norman Cousins had discovered that by watching funny films and reading humorous books he was able to control his arthritis very effectively. In fact, Cousins, who had discharged himself from hospital after being told that there was no cure, not only laughed himself better but also managed to obtain incontrovertible scientific proof that laughing had helped him to treat his arthritis. Peter was impressed by this, particularly when I pointed out to him that there didn't seem to be a lot of laughs in his life and that he rarely seemed to spend time with people who enjoyed having a good time.

He was, indeed, so impressed that he went out and rented a Marx Brothers video. It was, for him, a revelation. Peter had never, ever sat down and made time to watch something funny. He had never allowed himself to laugh before. But the Marx Brothers film converted him. The first sight of Harpo Marx, the first unwilling giggle, changed his life. Within weeks his arthritis was less troublesome than it had been for years. He discovered comedians he had never heard of before. I went in to his home one day and found a pile of videos which included films by Charlie Chaplin, Buster Keaton and Harold Lloyd as well as modern comics such as Chevy Chase and Robin Williams.

Peter's reading habits changed too. Instead of confining himself to tedious tomes about accountancy rules and taxation law he started to read humorists such as P. G. Wodehouse, James Thurber, Stephen Leacock, S. J. Perelman and Tom Sharpe.

Peter's arthritis didn't go away completely. And some days it still troubles him. But it is much, much better than it has been for years. He is able to move around far more easily than he had for years - and he doesn't need to take any tablets any more. For Peter, laughter really has proved to be the very best medicine.

What Else Can YOU Do To Help Overcome Rheumatoid Arthritis?

1. Lose Any Unnecessary Weight
Every pound of excess weight that you carry around with you puts an additional strain on all your joints, will make existing rheumatoid arthritis worse and will weaken otherwise healthy joints..

2. Give Up Meat

A vegetarian diet is more healthy if you are a sufferer from rheumatoid arthritis.

CHAPTER THREE:
OSTEOARTHRITIS

Introduction

Osteoarthritis usually first affects people in their fifties or six-ties. It seems to affect women slightly more often than men and in addition to the joints of the spine usually also affects the knees, hips, hands and feet. To start with there is usually only one joint affected but as time goes by osteoarthritis can spread to many parts of the body. Unlike rheumatoid arthritis (to which it bears remarkably few similarities other than that both are joint diseases) osteoarthritis does not involve damage to other parts of the body. Osteoarthritis is a much simpler disease to understand than rheumatoid arthritis. The main symptoms are stiffness and aching which develop as the cartilage between the bones gradually gets thinner and thinner. Eventually the bones end up rubbing on one another. Although osteoarthritis is often caused by excess wear and tear (in which case it is practically indistinguishable from the problems often caused by old age) it can be inherited and may affect younger adults.

What Are The Causes of Osteoarthritis?

We reach our physical peak in our late teens and early twenties and from then on it is, I'm afraid, all downhill! Our vision becomes less acute, our hearing more indistinct and our brains lose nerve cells at a frightening rate. Our bones become weaker and more likely to fracture, our muscles lose some of their strength and our joints stiffen up and start to creak a little. Most of these changes are gradual and painless and go unnoticed until we suddenly try to do something that we used to be able to do with ease and find that our bodies let us down.

It is the changes inside our joints which so often lead to

the development of osteoarthritis. As I have already explained a normal healthy joint is perfectly designed for the job it has to do. Those joints which have a synovium and which are filled with synovial fluid are particularly impressive from an engineering point of view: they are strong and they have a magnificently sophisticated, self-lubricating system. Each one of the synovial joints in a normal, healthy body is as slippery and as efficient as any man-made joint could ever hope to be.

Synovial joints have three special attributes:

* The synovial fluid inside the joint is made of a special substance which loses water and becomes thicker when the pressure on the joint is greater. This means that the lubricant automatically becomes more efficient and more protective when the need for lubrication is at its greatest.

* The two cartilaginous surfaces of a synovial joint are extraordinarily slippery and would move smoothly together even without a lubricant.

* Although the cartilaginous surfaces look smooth they are full of tiny indentations - rather like a golf ball. The result is that synovial fluid is trapped between the two surfaces - thereby reducing the amount of friction still further.

To get an idea of the amount of work each of your joints has to do just stop and think for a moment of the number of times that you move your arms and legs in a fairly ordinary sort of day. Getting up, sitting down and walking about all put a pressure on your joints. Obviously, all this action means that our joints must eventually begin to wear out. And that is often what happens as we get older. Our cartilages wear down and the production of lubricating fluid becomes a little sluggish.

But although osteoarthritis may be partly a consequence of ageing that is not by any means the whole story. For a start most of us are so accustomed to the fact that our joints are strong, resilient and hard wearing that we do very little to look after them or to help protect them from unnecessary wear and tear. The worst thing that most of us do to damage our joints is to allow ourselves to become overweight. If you are 14 pounds overweight then your joints will be constantly carrying an unnecessary load. Try picking up 14 pounds of sugar or flour and walking around with it for five minutes or so. That is what your joints have to put up with for every minute of your waking day. The heavier you are - and the more excess weight you are carrying - the greater the strain on your joints will be. If you are overweight then the chances are high that it will be the joints in your hips, knees and ankles - your weight bearing joints - which suffer from osteoarthritis first.

We make things even worse by taking exercise that puts a tremendous strain on our bodies, by battering our bones and our cartilages and by putting totally unreasonable demands on the resilience of our joints. When we are young our bones are resilient and capable of absorbing an enormous amount of stress. But as we age our bones become less elastic and less capable of taking any sort of punishment. The result is that your joints have to take increasing amounts of the shock when you walk, run, jump, dance or leap about. Your joints are at their best when you are about twenty years old. Every year after that means a year's additional decay. By the time you are thirty your joints may be noticeably stiffer and more vulnerable. After the age of forty weight bearing joints in particular are likely to start creaking and causing trouble. Jogging, running, tennis, squash, football and aerobics all put a tremendous strain on your joints (particularly if you are not wearing shock absorbing footwear). And, of course, if you are overweight then the strain will be increased even more.

Although osteoarthritis is usually a consequence of old age or over use it is not always a result of natural wear and tear. Sometimes osteoarthritis may develop in younger people who are not overweight and who have done relatively little exercise. When this happens it may be because salts have been deposited in the cartilages, because inflammation or infection has damaged the joint or because the two parts of a joint do not fit together properly as a result of some congenital abnormality (the hip joint is the one most commonly affected by congenital problems).

Who Gets Osteoarthritis?

Anyone can get osteoarthritis - at any age - but it doesn't usually start before the age of thirty or forty years old and it is commonest after the age of fifty. It affects women more than men and although it is so common that it is difficult to be certain about this it does seem to affect some families more than others. People who are overweight are prone to osteoarthritis and if you have ever had an injury in a joint then you will be more likely to get osteoarthritis in that joint.

How Common Is Osteoarthritis?

It is difficult to say how many people get osteoarthritis because most sufferers manage without seeking medical help but millions are disabled by osteoarthritis and it is probably the commonest cause of disability in the western world.

How Quickly Does Osteoarthritis Develop?

It is rare for osteoarthritis to develop quickly. It usually starts slowly and builds up gradually over a period of years. Often, osteoarthritis develops so slowly that a sufferer may become quite seriously crippled without ever really noticing or complaining of any severe pain or disablement. It is, however, possible for an injury (even a relatively minor one) to exacerbate or accelerate osteoarthritis in a joint.

Which Joints Does Osteoarthritis Affect?

Osteoarthritis normally only affects joints below the waist. The hips, knees, ankles, hands and feet are the joints most commonly affected. Sometimes some of the joints in the back may be affected. Occasionally, only one joint will be affected by osteoarthritis but it is more common for two or three joints to be involved.

The Hips
The hip is a ball and socket joint which has a wide range of movement (only the shoulder joint has a wider range) but because it is an important weight bearing joint it is the most common joint in the body to be affected by osteoarthritis. People who are overweight are particularly likely to be affected. When osteoarthritis develops in the hip it causes increasing stiffness and even the slightest movement may be painful. Walking can be very difficult and even movements in bed can cause excruciating pain. When a hip is affected by osteoarthritis it gradually changes in shape and the end result can be that the leg on that side may effectively become noticeably shorter than the other leg - making walking particularly difficult and putting an additional strain on the rest of the body. Because people who have damaged hips may be unable to move about enough to look after themselves properly osteoarthritis of the hip is by far the commonest single cause of disablement today.

The Knees
Osteoarthritis in the knees can cause a wide range of deformities. It can make the knees look knobbly. It can produce a 'bow legged' look or a 'knock-kneed' look. Patients with osteoarthritis of the knees often have difficulty in walking up and down stairs. The noises which osteoarthritis of the knees make are awful and it is possible to hear creaking and grating noises whenever osteoarthritic knee joints are moved.

The Ankles

Although they have to carry the weight of the whole body the ankles are less likely than the hips or knees to develop osteoarthritis - possibly because the normal range of movement in the ankle joint is less than the range of movement in the hips or knees and the amount of wear and tear is, therefore, considerably less. The ankle joint is only responsible for up and down movements of the foot - other movements (such as rotating and tilting) are produced by joints within the foot.

The Feet

The commonest joint in the foot to be affected by osteoarthritis is the joint at the base of the big toe. Problems at this joint are usually caused by long term pressure produced by shoes that don't fit properly. Women - who are more likely to wear tight shoes, high heeled shoes and shoes that are designed to look fashionable rather than to provide the feet with any protection or support - are far more likely to suffer from this particular type of osteoarthritis than men are.

The Shoulders

Only rarely affected by osteoarthritis - and usually only after injury.

The Elbows

Like the shoulders the elbows are only rarely affected by osteoarthritis - and, again, usually only after injury. The rarity of osteoarthritis in the shoulders and the elbows shows quite clearly just how important excess weight can be in the development of osteoarthritis of the knees and hips (which are joints of similar design and a similar range of movements).

The Hands

When osteoarthritis affects the hands it most commonly affects the joint at the base of the thumb and the joints at the ends of the fingers. Small, hard nodules often form at the backs of affected joints in the hand and although these are usually painless they can add to the stiffness of the joints.

What Are The Symptoms Of Osteoarthritis?

Pain is by far the most important symptom of osteoarthritis and can vary from a dull and persistent but often bearable ache to a sharp, gnawing pain. Usually worse after joints have been used a lot (that invariably means at the end of the day) the pain of osteoarthritis is produced when pain endings in the bones and ligaments are stimulated. The dull, deep and generalised ache in and around the affected joints is caused by changes in the pressure within the bones - which is itself a result of the failure of the joint to function properly. The sharper, more acute pain of osteoarthritis is usually produced when a ligament catches on or is stretched by a piece of irregular bone in the joint. In addition to these 'internal' pains there may sometimes be a feeling of tenderness over an affected joint.

The second significant symptom of osteoarthritis is stiffness which is usually worst in the mornings or after any period of rest or inactivity. Most sufferers of osteoarthritis find that their joints are worse if they spend a long time in the same position. Regular, gentle movements of a joint help to keep stiffness at bay although when a joint is affected by osteoarthritis its range of movement is usually less than the range of movement in a perfectly healthy joint.

Finally, there may be some swelling of osteoarthritic joints. In particular, nodules may appear around the finger joints and the knee joints may swell as fluid accumulates.

Osteoarthritis Is For Life

Osteoarthritis does not usually come and go and nor does it have 'active' and 'inactive' phases in the way that rheumatoid arthritis does. Usually, once a joint develops osteoarthritis it remains osteoarthritic for life.

Joint Damage May Result in Disablement

Osteoarthritis is a major cause of disablement. Since it is the knees and hips which are most commonly affected sufferers often have difficulty in walking, stooping, bending and stretching. They may also have difficulty in getting into and out of soft, 'comfortable' chairs.

Osteoarthritis Can Cause Inactivity and Depression

Because osteoarthritis causes disablement and makes mentally alert individuals immobile it commonly also causes depression.

What Tests Can Be Done For Osteoarthritis?

The X ray is the most important investigation. X ray pictures of suspected joints will show how much damage has been done, what changes there have been to the bones and whether there is any narrowing of the joint space between the bones. Blood tests are of limited value but doctors sometimes take a sample of fluid from a joint to check for any signs of inflammation and to look to see if there are any crystals present in the joint.

Can Osteoarthritis Be Treated?

Osteoarthritis cannot be 'cured' by any miracle pills (although surgeons can replace a damaged joint with a 'new' one) but there are many ways in which the symptoms can be controlled and the development of the disease can be minimised.

What Can Doctors Do?

Drugs

Drugs will not cure osteoarthritis nor will they affect the progress of the disease or prevent further damage, but drugs can help relieve pain and by relieving pain they can help you to keep your joints mobile and to avoid further stiffening developing. Pain killing drugs such as aspirin and paracetamol are the drugs most commonly used to give relief to sufferers from osteoarthritis and by relieving pain and combating inflammation they help reduce the amount of stiffness patients have to deal with. Many doctors also prescribe other drugs in the Non Steroidal Anti Inflammatory group but steroids are unlikely to be as useful in the treatment of osteoarthritis since it the symptoms are caused by physical wear and tear within the joint rather than by inflammation.

Injections

Injections can be performed to remove excess fluid and, if there is any inflammation in the joint, a steroid injection may be useful. However, since osteoarthritis is usually caused by wear and tear rather than inflammation steroid injections are unlikely to be as effective as they can be in the treatment of rheumatoid arthritis.

Surgery

Since the 1960s surgeons around the world have been replacing osteoarthritic hip joints with artificial joints and today hip replacement operations are commonplace and immensely successful. Indeed, hip replacement surgery has been so successful that many surgeons are now replacing other joints - particularly knees and joints in the hands.

The operation to remove and replace an osteoarthritic hip joint is relatively safe and straightforward to perform (it has been done on patients in their nineties). The osteoarthritic hip joint is simply removed and a metal and plastic replacement is glued into the patient's own bones. The success rate is high with most patients standing on their own feet a day or two after the operation and walking within two or three weeks. Advances are constantly being made in the design of joint replacements and, in particular, in the type of materials used to provide an effective long life replacement. It is, as you can imagine, difficult to mimic the efficiency of the human joint but artificial joints are being made which can last for fifteen years of fairly active movement.

Joint replacement is not the only type of surgery offered to patients with osteoarthritis. Sometimes it is possible to cut through the bone near to an osteoarthritic joint and to take pressure off the joint by realigning the bone. This sort of operation is called an osteotomy and in addition to removing pain and pressure from the area it can also stimulate the body to heal itself.

Physiotherapy
A physiotherapist can help to reduce pain and stiffness and to keep joints mobile.

Aids
If you are crippled or disabled in any way by osteoarthritis then you will undoubtedly be able to retain more of your independence by using some of the many available aids and appliances.(Some are described at the end of this book.)

What Can Alternative Or Complementary Therapists Do To Help Combat Osteoarthritis?

Because osteoarthritis is a disease which is usually caused by wear and tear within a joint (or joints) there is little that alternative or complementary therapists can do to provide permanent relief of symptoms. However, alternative and complementary therapists are often able to help relieve pain. Many patients have found that acupuncture is an extremely effective way of combating pain.

What Can You Do To Help Overcome Osteoarthritis?

Lose unnecessary weight

If you stop and think about it then it makes perfect sense that if you have arthritis of any kind you should try to lose any excess weight.

Osteoarthritis, which commonly affects large, weight bearing joints such as the hips and the knees is particularly likely to be made worse if you are overweight.

Sadly, of course, most of the people who try to lose weight fail. Even if they lose weight successfully in the short term most will put all their weight back on again within a few months. They fail because instead of changing their bad eating habits they try to lose weight by going on unnatural diets. Then, when they go back to their former eating habits, they simply put all the weight back on again.

If you are going to lose weight permanently then you really have to make sure that you change your eating habits permanently.

Here are two pieces of valuable advice which should help you lose your excess, unwanted weight - and keep it off!

1. Set Yourself A Manageable Target

Most slimmers start off by setting themselves impossible targets. They decide how much they need to lose and then aim at losing all of that excess weight - which they may have accumulated over a period of years - in just a few weeks. I once organised a survey of slimmers and discovered to my absolute horror that around nine out of every ten were aiming at a target weight that was far too low for them - worse still all of them were hoping to lose their weight at a completely unrealistic rate.

The problem with setting yourself an impossible target is that you will almost certainly fail. And then, when you fail, you will be depressed; you will think of yourself as a slimming failure and you will probably abandon your plans to lose weight. Failure breeds failure and once a would be slimmer has failed she (or he) will probably just give up, abandon all hope and put up with their excess weight.

So, the first thing you should do is to set yourself a realistic target.

Once you have decided roughly how much you should weigh you can, of course, simply subtract that from your current weight to find out how much you need to lose. Then, since you should aim at losing around two pounds a week, divide the total amount of weight you need to lose by two to find the number of weeks that your weight loss programme should last.

I know that this may sound a slow way of losing weight but even if you only lose two pounds a week you will be able to lose a massive 26 pounds (11.7 kilograms) in three months and 52 pounds (25.2 kilograms) in six months.

Once you've worked out your long term target, and obtained your doctor's permission to diet, give yourself some short term aims. Decide, for example, that you are going to try to lose eight pounds in the next month. And then weigh yourself just once a week to check on your progress. (Don't weigh yourself too often - your weight will fluctuate naturally from day to day and if you weigh yourself several times a day as some people do then you will probably depress yourself when you realise that your weight sometimes goes up a little when you think it ought to be going down).

The big advantage of this simple approach is that every time you hit a small and realistic slimming target you will think of yourself as a success. Every time you lose a bit more of your unwanted weight you will feel like a winner. And once you feel like a successful slimmer your confidence will be boosted and you will tackle your next slimming target with renewed enthusiasm.

2. Only Eat When You Are Hungry

There is an appetite control centre - an extremely impressive and powerful automatic device - hidden deep inside every human brain. The power of the appetite control centre is quite remarkable; it can make sure that you never become short of essential vitamins and minerals and it can make sure that you never weigh too much or too little.

All you have to do to take advantage of your appetite control centre is to learn to listen to it!

If you listen to your body - and you learn to eat when your body tells you to and to stop eating when it tells you to stop - then you will not go far wrong. If, in addition, you can make sure that you eat the foods your body tells you to eat you will not only stay slim but you will also stay healthy.

I have explained the virtues and values of this simple system to numerous slimmers and everyone who has had the small amount of determination it needs to try it out has succeeded - and has lost weight permanently. As far as I know there has never been a single failure.

This system is beautifully simple, it is foolproof, it doesn't cost any money, there are no side effects and it is permanent. It is hardly surprising if the only problem with it is that some people think it sounds too good to be true.

'Why,' ask the sceptics, 'am I fat if my brain already contains an appetite control centre that is supposed to keep me slim?'

There is a simple answer to that apparently difficult question.

The truth is that most of us have lost the art of listening to our own bodies. We have, sadly, acquired many bad eating habits and we allow these to overrule our internal appetite control centre.

We eat for all sorts of 'bad' reasons.

We eat not because we are hungry but because we are bored (and food provides us with excitement); because we are depressed (and eating cheers us up) and because we are guilty (and food helps us to forget our guilt). We eat at fixed meal times (whether we are hungry or not) because we have been taught to eat at fixed meal times. We finish up all the food on our plates (whether or not we need it) because when we were small we were told about the starving millions - and reminded that they would be grateful for the food we were leaving. We eat more than we need because when we were bottle fed our mothers taught us to empty the bottle - rather than to listen to our own appetite control centres telling us that we were full.

And so it goes on.

Over the years we acquire many bad eating habits. We ignore our appetite control centres. And so it is hardly surprising that we end up getting fat.

The single, most important secret of permanent slimming success is to eat when you are hungry - and to stop eating when you are no longer hungry.

The Twenty Five Top Slimming Tips

1. *Give up eating meals.* Eating five or six small snacks instead of three large meals will help your body adjust its intake to its needs. People who 'snack' lose weight much more success-fully than people who over-fill themselves with food three or four times a day.

2. *Stand up for yourself.* Don't let other people decide what you eat (or when you eat it). If you're full - say so!

3. *Set yourself easy slimming targets.* Slimmers who try to get rid of all their excess weight in a month will fail - as will peo-ple who try to lose too much weight. Decide what your ideal weight should be and then aim at losing two pounds a week.

4. *Only ever eat when you are hungry.* And stop when you are full. Every time you are about to put food into your mouth ask

yourself whether or not you really need it.

5. *Don't eat in the evening.* If you eat when you're sitting down - or about to go to bed - your body will store the unwanted food as fat. You should do most of your eating early in the day - so that your body can burn up the food.

6. *Start a compost heap.* Never be afraid to throw food away if you don't want it. Most people who have a weight problem hate seeing food wasted and will finish up the scraps off other peoples' plates rather than dump unwanted food into the bin.

7. *Take regular exercise.* It will help tone up your muscles and burn up extra energy. Swimming and walking are both excellent and stress free.

8. *Don't worry about weighing food.* Allow your body to help you diet successfully by deciding when - and how much - you need to eat.

9. *Don't feed hunger immediately.* If you feel hungry and find yourself reaching for food wait five minutes. Then - if you still feel hungry - you can eat.

10. *Don't start eating too soon.* When you sit down to a meal do not immediately start shovelling food into your mouth. Sit for a moment or two and relax. Try to get rid of accumulated tensions. Then eat slowly and concentrate on what you are doing. This way you will be far more likely to hear your body 'talking' to you.

11. *Stop between courses and rest.* If you've had enough to eat get up and leave the table. Never stay sitting at the table after you've finished eating or else there is a risk that you will nibble at whatever is left.

12. *Use sweeteners instead of sugar.*

13. *Never reward yourself with food.* If you are pleased or proud or you want to celebrate do so with a bunch of flowers, a new tape or a book or magazine. Food is for eating.

14. *Don't spend too much time looking at mouth watering food.* There is evidence now to show that you can get fat just by looking. When you see, smell or think of food your body starts

to prepare its digestive processes. Saliva is released in your mouth and your stomach produces juices to help digest the coming food. The pancreas is stimulated and insulin is produced. The insulin then starts to convert the glucose in your bloodstream into fat as your body clears the way for the food it thinks is on the way. However, as the amount of sugar in your blood falls so you will begin to feel genuinely hungry. And you will need to eat. Your body will have been tricked by its own senses.

15. *Don't weigh yourself every day.* Once a week is enough. Your weight will vary daily for all sorts of reasons and you are likely to become obsessed or depressed if you weigh yourself too often.

16. *Don't diet alone.* If you find slimming alone too difficult, consider joining a slimming club. There are hundreds of them around. Look in the local telephone book or ask your doctor. Many people get support and encouragement from slimming with others.

17. *Examine your bad habits.* Spend a little time working out how you acquired your bad eating habits. What bad eating habits did you learn as a child? Awareness of your bad eating habits will make them easier to conquer.

18. *Eat most of your meals sitting at the table.* Never eat in front of the TV set. You need to concentrate on what you are doing if you are going to use the power of your mind to help you slim successfully. Do not carry food around your home - eat only in the kitchen or dining room.

19. *Avoid "special" slimming diets.* Do not follow any 'magical' or 'wonder' diets that promise you instant slenderness. And don't waste your money on slimming pills or supplements.

20. *Watch out for celebrations.* If you have to attend a big dinner or celebration meal and you are worried that it will ruin your diet have a snack half an hour beforehand. It will spoil your appetite and ensure that you feel full long before you do your diet too much damage.

21. *Don't be a food "tester".* Try to resist the temptation to

taste food when you are preparing it. Many cooks kid themselves that they are testing food as they cook. But by the time the meal is ready they have eaten far more than a 'sample'. This sort of eating has nothing to do with hunger - and is probably one of the reasons why so many people who work in the catering industry are overweight.

22. *Don't eat by the clock.* Remember that you don't have to have a cup of coffee and a biscuit just because it is break-time. Instead of eating why not read a magazine, write a letter or make a telephone call?

23. *Throw out your old clothes.* When you have lost weight, throw out the clothes that no longer fit you. If you keep them then you are admitting that you do not expect your weight loss to be permanent.

24. *Check the effects of drugs.* Many prescribed pills can produce an unwanted weight gain. Drugs such as steroids can do this, for example. If you taking any prescribed drug talk to your doctor and ask him if he thinks it could affect your ability to lose weight. There may be an alternative drug that your doctor can prescribe.

25. *Eat rice!* It is an excellent - and in the West often underused - food. Brown rice is filling and full of nourishment. It makes a good alternative to potatoes. Wholewheat pasta, too, is another underused food in many homes.

Case history

Enid had suffered from osteoarthritis for seven years and during that time she had steadily put on weight.

When I first saw her she weighed four stones more than she should have done and she found walking so difficult and so painful that she rarely moved out of her home. She looked ten years older than she was.

In the mornings she would lie in bed until her husband helped her up. Then she would spend most of the day sitting in an easy chair by the fire. Because she did not go out she lost interest in her appearance and she let herself go. She never bothered with her hair, she never wore make up and she invariably wore the same colourless, shapeless and rather grubby clothes.

Inevitably, because she was bored, she spent much of her time eating. And because she took very little exercise to burn up the food which she was consuming she steadily put on weight. Her life had become a vicious circle: her osteoarthritis made it difficult for her to move; she ate more than her body needed; she put on weight; and as she put on the extra weight so she found movement ever more painful.

I persuaded Enid to try to lose weight. Within a month she had lost over half a stone and within three months she had lost two stones! Most important of all she had lost this weight not by going on a short term diet but by changing her eating habits and her attitude to food. To her delight she found that without the excess weight to carry around she could walk and move far more easily. Her osteoarthritis had not changed but without so much excess weight to carry her joints were far less painful when she walked.

Today Enid is unrecognisable. She looks ten years younger than her real age. She and her husband go out together several evenings a week and occasionally she has even tried a little old-fashioned ballroom dancing.

Dieting has changed Enid's life!

Learn To Relax
When muscles are tightened and tensed by stress joints will suffer more than when muscles are loose and relaxed.

Learn How To Deal With Pain

Pain is the single most important symptom associated with osteoarthritis. Although drugs such as aspirin can be extremely effective in helping to combat pain there are many other techniques for controlling pain. (See Chapter Five.)

Exercise Whenever You Can

Regular exercise will help to keep joints loose and supple. If you spend too long keeping still (to prevent discomfort) you will find that your joints are much worse when you eventually have to move. Combating osteoarthritis is a compromise: when your joints are sore or painful and when movement hurts then you should rest, but when you can move you should. A regular exercise programme should push all your joints (including those not yet affected by the disease) through a full range of movements. But you must consult your doctor and obtain his approval before you begin any exercise programme.

Build Up Your Self-Confidence

Sufferers from osteoarthritis are, like sufferers from rheumatoid arthritis, likely to lack self-confidence.

Learn To Let Your Feelings Show

Holding in anger and sadness will make your osteoarthritis far worse. You will benefit enormously if you can let your emotions show.

Learn To Laugh

Laughter probably won't help osteoarthritis sufferers as much as it will help patients with rheumatoid arthritis. But I believe it can help.

Give Up Eating Meat

A vegetarian diet seems to help patients with arthritis - though whether it helps non inflammatory types of arthritis such as osteoarthritis as much as it helps inflammation disorders such as rheumatoid arthritis is open to question. However, I firmly believe that a meat-free diet is generally healthier than a diet which includes meat.

CHAPTER FOUR:
OTHER ARTHRITIC DISORDERS

Introduction

Rheumatoid arthritis and osteoarthritis are, without a doubt, the two commonest and most important arthritic disorders. But they are not the only arthritic disorders. As I have already explained there are well over one hundred other types of arthritis - far too many to discuss them all in detail here. In this chapter I will describe the commonest and most important of the other arthritic disorders. Many of the treatment techniques I have already described in chapters two and three are effective in the control of these disorders and in the relief of symptoms and many of the techniques described in later chapters are also useful. Please talk to your own doctor and ask for his advice about which treatments will be most useful for you. You should not try anything new without first obtaining your doctor's permission.

Ankylosing Spondylitis

Joints involved:
The joints of the spine, particularly the lower back are the ones most commonly affected but sometimes the larger joints of the body (the hips, knees and shoulders) also become inflamed and stiffen up. 'Spondylitis' means inflammation of the spine and 'ankylosing' means stiffening. Although the disease tends to start at the bottom of the spine it usually travels upwards over a period of years.

Usually affects:
The most common sufferers are young, white males, between the ages of 15 and 25 - but women can be affected. Ankylosing spondylitis tends to run in families.

Caused by:
The stiffness is caused by an inflammation where the ligaments are attached to bones but just what causes this inflammation is still a mystery. Ankylosing spondylitis may be inherited (it is definitely associated with a particular gene) and may be caused by an infection or some other environmental factor. Ankylosing spondylitis is quite different to rheumatoid arthritis (another inflammatory disorder). In rheumatoid arthritis the inflammation is inside the joints but in ankylosing spondylitis the inflammation affects the edges of the joints. As time goes by the inflamed joint edges turn into bone - and it is this that causes the stiffness. Eventually, the new bone may join two vertebrae together completely so that part of the back becomes completely rigid.

Symptoms
Pain and stiffness in the back and any other joints involved are the first and most obvious symptoms. If a nerve is trapped there may be pain going down the back of the leg. These symptoms are usually worse in the mornings and after resting and they are relieved by exercise. The symptoms gradually get worse and worse as time goes by - with the patient becoming stiffer and finding bending increasing difficult. There is also sometimes inflammation of the eye(s), the skin and other parts of the body. Ankylosing spondylitis tends to burn itself out around the age of fifty or so as the inflammation becomes less intense.

How common is it?
Ankylosing spondylitis is the third most common form of arthritis (after osteoarthritis and rheumatoid arthritis). It affects between 1 in 200 and 1 in 400 people.

Treatment
Regular exercise is vitally important since it can help to delay stiffening of the spine. For the same reason physiotherapy is

also important. Drugs normally used in the treatment of rheumatoid arthritis and osteoarthritis are sometimes used to help control the pain and stiffness associated with ankylosing spondylitis.

Gout

Joints involved:
Any joint in the body can be affected but the big toes are the ones most commonly involved. The ankles, knees, wrists, elbows and fingers are also common sites for gout.

Usually affects:
Men rather than women (in a ratio of 20 to 1). Gout usually affects individuals between the ages of 35 and 60 and it runs in families. Most gout sufferers are rather overweight and often also have high blood pressure.

Caused by:
Gout develops when the levels of uric acid in the blood get too high and uric acid crystals accumulate in the joints. Normally, uric acid is formed when waste products are broken down in the body. In a healthy individual the uric acid is excreted in the urine but gout sufferers fail to get rid of all the uric acid their bodies are making. There are several possible reasons for this. The kidneys may not be damaged - and not getting rid of uric acid properly. There may be an inherited tendency to high levels or uric acid. Or the problem may simply be caused by eating too many foods which are broken down to produce high levels of uric acid. Prescribed drugs can sometimes trigger a high uric acid level - and an attack of gout.

Symptoms:
Gout usually begins with a fairly sudden onset of severe pain in a joint which is usually swollen and rather bluish red in colour.

There may also be a moderate fever. The symptoms of gout tend to come and go quite unexpectedly. The first attack of gout usually begins with an itchy, swollen toe which gradually becomes painful. If gout is untreated it may eventually lead to joint damage - producing long term symptoms rather similar to those associated with osteoarthritis.

How common is it?
Fairly common - probably similar in incidence to ankylosing spondylitis. But many sufferers only get one or two attacks a year.

Treatment:
Patients with acute gout are usually advised to rest. Anti-inflammatory drugs are sometimes prescribed to ease pain and some patients need long term treatment with drugs which prevent the accumulation of uric acid or which help the kidneys to get rid of uric acid and which thereby help to prevent pain recurring. Many patients notice an improvement in their condition if they lose weight and avoid certain foods or drugs. Foods which are particularly likely to cause problems include: meat extracts, game, asparagus, spinach, strawberries, rhubarb, fish roe, herring, salmon, whitebait, liver, kidneys and sweetbreads. Drinks which can cause gout include: carbonated drinks, beer, sparkling wines, port, champagne and may other kinds of alcohol. Treatment of gout is important because if uric acid levels are allowed to remain high the kidneys may be damaged by an accumulation of crystals.

Juvenile Rheumatoid Arthritis

Joints involved:
There are several different types of juvenile rheumatoid arthritis but the small joints of the fingers, toes, wrists and ankles are the ones most commonly affected. The neck, shoulders, hip and knees may also be involved.

Usually affects:
Children of any age can be affected but juvenile arthritis affects girls more often than boys. It most commonly starts either very early (between the ages of two and four) or just before or around puberty.

Caused by:
Very little is known about the cause of juvenile rheumatoid arthritis although it does appear to be inherited.

Symptoms
The illness usually begins with a high fever and most sufferers start feeling unwell before any joint problems appear. Children with juvenile rheumatoid arthritis may fail to grow properly, may lose weight and may complain of abdominal pains. The heart, liver, spleen and lymph nodes may be affected, the eyes may be inflamed and there may also be a skin rash. The joint symptoms may not start until the disease has been present for several months.

How common is it?
Quite rare.

Treatment
Three quarters of childhood sufferers from juvenile rheumatoid arthritis recover completely. Careful exercise, the splinting of affected joints to protect them, physiotherapy and rest all help. Children are usually advised to avoid contact sports which might result in joint injury. Both drugs and surgery are sometimes used.

Polymyalgia Rheumatica

Joints involved:
The hips and shoulders, thighs and neck are most commonly

affected.

Usually affects:
Polymyalgia rheumatica can affect both men and women but affects two or three times as many women as men. It doesn't usually affect anyone under the age of 50.

Caused by:
The cause of the pain and discomfort associated with polymyalgia rheumatica is unknown.

Symptoms:
The main symptoms of polymyalgia rheumatica are tenderness and discomfort in the hips, shoulders and neck. The discomfort is usually at its worst early on in the morning, gradually getting worse later on in the day. Many patients have difficulty in getting out of bed. Patients often also complain of depression, tiredness, weakness, weight loss and fever. The symptoms may develop gradually or suddenly.

How common is it?
Uncommon

Treatment:
Steroids usually provide dramatic relief. Indeed, the results are so spectacular that giving steroids is sometimes regarded as a diagnostic test for this disease.

Psoriatic Arthritis

Joints involved:
Psoriasis is a fairly common skin disease in which patches of skin become inflamed, red and scaly. Psoriatic arthritis can affect any joint in the body but is usually restricted to just one or two joints. The joints near to the finger tips are particularly

likely to be affected.

Usually affects:
Psoriatic arthritis affects one in ten psoriasis sufferers.

Caused by:
No one really understands the link between psoriasis and arthritis (although there are lots of theories). It seems likely, however, that both skin and joints are affected by inflammation.

Symptoms:
The symptoms depend upon the type of arthritis that develops. Some patients develop symptoms similar to rheumatoid arthritis (although the symptoms tend to be less severe. Others get ankylosing spondylitis. Individual joints - particular in the fingers and toes may be affected or the disease may flare up intermittently in different joints around the body. Psoriatic arthritis tends to be even more unpredictable than other forms of arthritis.

How common is it?
Psoriasis affects approximately one in fifty people. And one in ten of those get psoriatic arthritis.

Treatment:
The treatment of the joint symptoms will depend upon the type of arthritis involved. Usually skin and joint problems are treated separately because the powerful drugs which can treat both problems are likely to produce unpleasant side effects.

Reactive Arthritis

Joints involved:
The joints of the legs - knees, ankles and feet - are affected more commonly than any other.

Usually affects:
Men are affected more than women and young adults (between 18 and 35) are the group most likely to suffer.

Caused by:
Reactive arthritis is triggered by an infection of the bowel or urinary tract. Sometimes the trigger is a sexually transmitted infection.

Symptoms:
The joints affected are likely to develop arthritic type symptoms but in addition to an inflammation of the joints there is likely to be an inflammation of the eyes, skin and mouth. Patients usually complain of sore eyes, skin rashes, pain on passing urine and mouth ulcers as well as the joint symptoms.

How common is it?
Uncommon.

Treatment:
Treatment will depend very much on the symptoms. The infection which has caused the generalised inflammation will probably need treating first of all but if the joints are badly affected anti inflammatory drugs may be needed. If fluid has accumulated in the joints some of it may need to be drawn off. Painful joints may need rest. Reactive arthritis does not usually produce any long term damage.

Rheumatic Fever

Joints involved:
Rheumatic fever affects large joints such as the knees but moves from joint to joint - rarely affecting any one joint for more than a few days.

Usually affects:
Children between the ages of 5 and 15.

Caused by:
The disease starts as a throat infection which triggers a complex immune response within the body.

Symptoms:
Patients usually complain of a persistent fever and pains which flit from joint to joint. As soon as one joint recovers another becomes affected. The joints are swollen, painful and hot. There is usually a history of a sore throat some two weeks or so before the joint pains develop. The arthritic symptoms normally last a few weeks. The most dangerous aspect of rheumatic fever is that about one half of all patients who contract the disease develop heart trouble - though the evidence of the damage may not become apparent for several years. Rheumatic fever may also cause a skin rash and small lumps in the skin. If the nervous system is affected the patient may develop irregular, uncontrollable, jerky movements.

How common is it?
Rare in developed countries but still common in Asia and Africa.

Treatment:
Rest is vitally important. Penicillin is normally needed to deal with the infection. Aspirin is the most effective pain killer. If the heart valves are affected heart surgery may be needed later on.

Rheumatism

Rheumatism is not a disease but a word used to describe just about any type of ache or pain affecting a bone, joint or muscle.

Septic Arthritis

Joints involved:
Any joint can be affected.

Usually affects:
Septic arthritis can affect anyone but is particularly likely to affect patients already suffering from rheumatoid arthritis or diabetes. It is also a possible complication of injections into a joint or surgery on or around a joint. Because it lowers the body's immune response to infection steroid treatment makes septic arthritis more likely.

Caused by:
A variety of organisms can cause a joint infection.

Symptoms:
The joint involved is usually painful, swollen, hot and very tender. Joint movement is limited. There is usually a fever too.

How common is it?
Fairly common.

Treatment:
Antibiotics are usually needed to overcome the infection. The joint may need to be drained.

CHAPTER FIVE:
THE CONTROL OF PAIN

Introduction

Whatever sort of arthritis you suffer from pain is more likely to cause misery, unhappiness and despair than all your other symptoms put together. When left untreated or badly treated, pain leads to physical and mental exhaustion, to disablement and to chronic depression. Patients with persistent pain need to spend long periods in bed and are far more likely to develop other serious medical complications. Patients with pain get better more slowly and need more support from friends, family and professionals.

Sadly, the pain caused by arthritis is not always treated well and many doctors tell patients who are suffering from arthritis pain simply to 'take things easy' or to 'grit their teeth and be brave'. Too often doctors turn to drug treatment as a first line of attack, not necessarily because drugs are best but because they will have received all their post graduate training from drug companies anxious to sell their products.

For many years researchers have been searching for, identifying and testing new ways of dealing with pain. Many of the techniques they have discovered are safe, effective and inexpensive. But the drug companies have no interest in non drug therapies and so the majority of practising doctors, who get much of their education from drug company sponsored literature, continue to ignore these treatments. Read the rest of this chapter carefully. You will, I hope, find some of the pain relieving techniques I have explained exciting and useful.

What Is Pain?

The whole story of just how pain reaches your brain has long mystified scientists. The traditional theory, first made popular by Descartes in 1664, was that when a pain receptor is stimulated the pain message travels straight up to the brain. Descartes believed that it was all very simple - rather like a campanologist tugging on a bell rope to start the church bells ringing.

This theory was popular with doctors until fairly recently and many believed that in cases of intractable, long term pain it would help to cut the nerves carrying the pain impulses up to the brain.

Unfortunately, this old-fashioned theory doesn't stand up very well. One major problem is that cutting the nerve doesn't stop pain impulses getting through. Indeed, it may make the pain worse. A second problem is the fact that pain can continue long after the original stimulus has been removed. A third is that pain can occur spontaneously and may spread to apparently unrelated parts of the body. And, finally, there is the problem that psychological factors can interfere quite dramatically with pain perception. Under some circumstances awful stimuli seem to produce no perceptible pain at all. Whereas under other circumstances modest stimulations can produce terrible pain. If we try to stick with the simple 'bell rope' theory of pain none of this makes any sense at all.

Then, in 1965 a psychologist called Ronald Melzack and an anatomist called Patrick Wall produced their 'gate control theory' which revolutionised the way doctors thought about pain. Melzack and Wall claimed that only a certain amount of sensory information can be processed by the nervous system at any one time and that when too much information tries to get through the limited number of junctions in the spinal cord result in some of the signals being shut out. The theory is that there is, in the spinal cord, a mechanism rather like a garden gate. The gate can only accept a limited number of messages through at any one time and if too many messages try to get through at once then the gate becomes blocked.

The gate control theory rests upon the fact that messages

arrive at the spinal cord in three quite separate ways. First, there are the two main types of nerve fibre which detect pain and other sensations and which carry electrical impulses produced by the receptors in the body's muscles and other tissues. The thicker of these two types of fibre carry sensations such as touch and pressure while the other, thinner fibres carry pain messages. These two fibres differ in various ways. First, the thinner fibres can regrow if they are damaged whereas the thicker fibres cannot regenerate and tend to diminish in number over the years. The second, and much more important difference, is that the thicker fibres carry their nervous impulses much more rapidly than the thinner fibres do. In addition to the messages travelling up towards your brain there are, of course, also likely to be instructions travelling down from the brain towards your muscles and other tissues.

Under normal circumstances the junctions or 'gates' in your spinal cord can carry these three different types of message quite comfortably but if too many impulses reach the spinal cord the 'gates' just cannot cope: they shut down and won't accept any more messages at all. It is this inability of the cells in the spinal cord to cope with the number of messages they are getting which explains why some stimuli produce far more savage pains than other apparently comparable stimuli. It also explains how simply rubbing a sore or injured area can help get rid of the pain.

Imagine again that you have carelessly hit your thumb with your hammer. Your instinct will be to rub the thumb vigorously. There will now be two sorts of impulses racing along your nerves to try to get into your spinal cord and up to your brain: pain impulses, travelling along the thinner nerve fibres, and touch impulses, travelling along the thicker nerve fibres.

Inevitably, the 'gate' will be blocked and some impulses will be unable to get through. And since the touch impulses are travelling faster than the pain impulses they will get there first. Most of the pain impulses will be unable to get through.

Rubbing a sore or damaged area is a natural response designed to stimulate the sending of simple 'sensation' messages and thereby blocking the passage of pain messages.

There is another way in which the 'gate' can be blocked.

If enough messages are coming down from the brain towards the tissues then the 'gate' will be blocked from the other side and, once again, the pain messages won't be able to get through. So, if you are concentrating very hard on what you are doing with your hammer you may not even notice that you've hit yourself until much later when you see the bruising! This is, of course, why you can work in the garden and get scratched without being aware of it and why you can cut yourself in the kitchen without realising it. It is why a footballer can carry on playing even though he has a broken neck, how a soldier can carry on fighting even though his foot has been shot off, why a man can pick up his severed arm and walk calmly with it to the nearest hospital. (All true stories). And it also why two young lovers can stand outside in the freezing cold without noticing that they are getting frostbitten.

Of course, if the number of impulses travelling along the smaller fibres and carrying the pain messages greatly exceeds the number of fast moving messages travelling along the larger fibres and the messages coming down from the brain then the pain message will get through the 'gate' and you will become aware of the pain.

The 'gate control' theory helps to explain why pain is such an unpredictable force. And it shows why 'alternative' pain control techniques can be so effective.

The Conquering Of Pain - The TENS Machine

Having realised just how rubbing a sore or painful place can relieve pain the next step for scientists was to come up with a way of stimulating the passage of non painful sensations even more efficiently. And the experts came up with the idea of using electricity to produce the necessary stimulus.

After various experiments it was discovered that by giving patients small pocket sized devices which sent out a series of electrical pulses the passage of pain messages could be blocked. The technique was called Transcutaneous Electrical Nerve Stimulation and the devices which were used were called TENS machines. It was quickly found that in addition to sending sensory messages which blocked the passage of pain impulses the TENS machines also encouraged the body to produce its own endorphins or pain relieving hormones.

Numerous studies have shown that patients with disorders such as arthritis can benefit enormously from using TENS machines. There are very few side effects - and the machines cost relatively little to buy (compared to the cost of a year's supply of pain killers they are a very good buy).

If you want to try a TENS machine talk to your own doctor. Although many members of the medical profession are still unaware of the existence or usefulness of TENS machines (largely because most doctors still get most of their post graduate education from drug companies) a growing number are learning about them. If your own doctor has never heard of these extremely effective devices ask him to arrange for you to see a consultant at your local hospital or, alternatively, ask him to refer you to the nearest specialist pain clinic.

Know How - and When - To Rest

It is a mistake to rest too much. If you suffer regularly from sore or painful joints you should try to keep as active as you possibly can and you should try to move your joints whenever they are not painful.

The danger is that if you rest too much then both your body and your mind will stagnate; your muscles will become weak and flabby (and you will run a greater than usual risk of falling when you do try to walk or move about) and your mind will slow down. But, having said all that, there is absolutely no doubt that there are times when rest is important. And it is vitally important that as an arthritis sufferer you know when to rest and how to rest.

First, the when.

You must learn to recognise when your body really needs rest, and when too much activity will make your pain worse rather than better. The most important thing to remember is that whenever you have an acute or sudden attack of pain you should make sure that you rest. Do not try to be brave or a 'hero' for if you do then the chances are that you will damage your joints even more. You should always avoid doing anything which makes your pain worse or which seems to make your condition worse in any other way. This does not, however, mean that you should never move any part of your body that feels uncomfortable. Many arthritis sufferers are never really free of discomfort. It is vital to keep moving those joints which are sore for if you do not move them there is a real danger that they will deteriorate even further. You should try to differentiate between genuine and threatening pain (which means that you should rest as much as you can) and modest and bearable discomfort (when you can move without creating extra pain).

You should also be prepared to rest whenever you feel tired or worn out. Some arthritis sufferers who have heard that patients who do not move will become 'fixed' in one position and permanently disabled, are so determined to keep mobile and active that they force themselves to keep moving all the time - even when they are totally exhausted.

As I have already explained it is important to keep active and busy but if you try to force your body to do too much by pushing yourself more and more then you will exhaust your reserves and you will, ironically, increase your susceptibility to pain. It is vitally important that you learn to recognise your limits. You must be prepared to take a break when you feel that your body needs a rest.

In addition to learning when to rest you must also learn how to rest so that your body benefits. For example, it is extremely important that you do not succumb to the temptation to put pillows under sore joints and to hold uncomfortable limbs in fixed positions. There is a real risk that if you do this then your joint will become fixed and quite immobile in an entirely impractical and very difficult position. It is important never to forget that painful joints can stiffen up very quickly indeed. As well as taking short breaks when your joints are stiff and painful you should also try to take longer term breaks when you can. Like everyone else arthritis sufferers are vulnerable to stress and pressure and anxiety and when exposed to problems their general health will usually suffer.

Inevitably, when your general health suffers your joints will become more painful. So taking regular breaks away from your everyday stresses and worries is an important part of your treatment and pain control programme. You don't have to travel abroad or go anywhere expensive, of course. These days it can often be cheaper to spend a few days out of season at the seaside than it is to stay at home. Try to make sure that you go somewhere peaceful and relaxing where you can unwind and escape from pressure. Remember that if your body needs a break then your mind almost certainly needs a break too.

Hidden Influences - Factors Which Affect The Pain You Feel

Have you ever come in from the garden, got into the bath and discovered that your arms and legs are covered in scratches and bruises? Have you ever been busy in the kitchen and then suddenly noticed that there is blood everywhere - from a finger you didn't even know you'd cut? Have you ever been for a long walk, arrived home tired but happy and then woken up next day feeling stiff and hardly able to move? In all those instances pain impulses - telling you to stop -just couldn't get through the 'gate' because you were engrossed in what you were doing and messages coming down from your brain telling your body what to do were blocking the pathways and leaving no room for pain messages.

I have already described how pain impulses travel to your brain - and can get held up. But there are other ways in which pain impulses can be hidden or arrested en route to your brain. Most important of all is the fact that for a pain to be felt the stimulus must exceed your personal pain threshold. If you are going to be aware that you have hit your thumb you must hit it with a certain amount of force. If you hit your thumb a light, glancing blow then you might be aware that your thumb has been 'touched' but you won't feel a 'pain'. You have to hit your thumb with a certain amount of force if your tissues are going to stimulate a nervous 'pain' response.

Pain thresholds vary from one indvidual to another. But, more important still, your pain threshold varies from minute to minute according to a variety of hidden factors. Here are some of them:

Your attitude towards your pain:
If you think a pain is trivial and harmless you will ignore it and it will probably go away. If you think a pain is serious and potentially life threatening you will worry about it and it will not go away. Your attitude towards the pain can be more important than the strength of the pain itself.

Where you are and what you are doing:
During a football match not long ago one of the goal-keepers broke his neck. But he carried on playing! He was so wrapped up in the game that he ignored his pain until the match had finished. Then he realised that he'd done something serious. If you're busy with an important tennis match you won't notice the blisters on your hand. If you're trying to reach succulent

blackberries in a hedge you won't notice the scratches you get trying to reach them. Your ability to tolerate pain goes up dramatically when you are busy doing something that holds your attention. In one experiment volunteers found that they could put up with extra pain if they listened to music they liked.

How frightened you are:
Have you ever had toothache, booked an appointment to see the dentist and found that by the time you walked into the consulting room your pain had disappeared? You aren't alone if you have. It is very common. When you are first aware of an aching tooth your threshold is low. You are worried by the pain and you don't know how long it is going to last. Fear lowers your pain threshold and pain tolerance levels. As soon as you've got your appointment to see the dentist your anxiety begins to lift. You feel more confident. And because you know that relief will soon be available you suffer less from the pain.

Whether you are depressed:
Have you ever had a day when everything seems to go wrong? If you have then you know that by the end of it the smallest problem can become a crisis. A lost button, a missed bus or a mislaid pen can all seem horrendous. Small difficulties get taken out of all proportion when we feel low. Your response to pain is influenced by mood in exactly the same way. If you are feeling unhappy and you hit your thumb then the pain will seem worse than if you are feeling happy when you hit your thumb.

Your sex:
Women have much the same sort of pain threshold as men but they are less tolerant of pain than men. This is probably because men are taught to be 'strong' and not to cry out when it pain. On average men can tolerate pain for 20% longer than women.

The number of brothers and sisters you have:
Children who grow up with at least three other brothers and sisters are likely to have much higher pain tolerance levels than children who grow up with fewer brothers and sisters. Children with no brothers or sisters at all are likely to grow up with lower pain threshold and pain tolerance levels than anyone else.

Your age:
Your ability to tolerate pain will change as you get older. You will become better able to tolerate superficial pains and less able to tolerate deep pains.

Your nationality:
Italians and Indians have a low pain tolerance level while the English have a high pain tolerance level. Jews are less capable of coping with pain than Gentiles while North Europeans and Americans of North European extraction are better able to cope with pain than people from other countries. White skinned individuals tend to be better at tolerating pain than blacks. The Japanese and the Chinese are least capable of coping with pain.

What you learned as a child:
Children are influenced by their parents. If your parents made a fuss every time you got a knock or a bruise then you will have a comparatively low pain threshold and pain tolerance level. If, however, your parents took little notice when you complained of pain then you will have grown up indifferent to pain - with a high pain threshold and a great ability to tolerate pain. Children can 'learn' pain behaviour from their parents. If you grew up in a household where one or both parents complained of back trouble you are more likely to suffer from back pain.

What Is The Difference Between Pain Threshold and Pain Tolerance?

Your pain threshold level is the point at which you start to notice pain. Your pain tolerance level is the amount of pain you can stand.

How To Measure Your Pain

It is impossible to measure pain objectively. There are so many different factors involved that it is impossible for you to compare the pain you get in your joints with the pain your neighbour gets in her womb. But you can measure variations in a particular pain. You can tell whether or not a specific pain is getting better or worse. And by doing this you can tell whether or not a pain relieving technique that you are using is working.

Look through the list of words which follow and pick out the four which you think describe your pain most accurately:

      sore (1)
      dull (1)
      tender (1)
      annoying (1)
      troublesome (1)
      uncomfortable (1)
      tiring (2)
      hurting (2)
      heavy (2)
      distressing (2)
      miserable (2)
      sickening (2)
      exhausting (3)
      frightful (3)
      wretched (3)
      intense (3)

horrible (3)
punishing (3)
terrifying (4)
vicious (4)
killing (4)
unbearable (4)
excruciating (4)
intolerable (4)

Add up the numbers that follow each of the four words you have chosen. The total is your 'pain score'.

Next time you want to measure your pain look through the list again and repeat the procedure, comparing your total score with previous total scores.

Try To Dominate Your Pain

Anyone who suffers from constant (or near constant) pain will confirm that before long the pain begins to take over. Many arthritis sufferers have confirmed to me that their pains and infirmities rule their lives and their relationships with other people.

'It started quite innocuously,' said one arthritis victim. 'When I first developed bad arthritis my wife was very kind and understanding. She made a fuss of me and looked after me and gradually started to do more and more things for me. She fetched things for me. If I dropped the paper she picked it up for me. If I wanted some pipe tobacco she walked to the corner shop and I let her. I let her because it was quicker for her to do things and I didn't have to make any effort. But eventually I realised that our relationship had changed. Instead of treating me like a partner she was treating me like a child. By then our relationship had changed permanently and it was too late to go back. In the end my arthritis ruined my marriage and resulted in my divorce.'

If you suffer from bad arthritis and you find it difficult to move and get about you will almost certainly find that the people who are close to you will want to help you. Friends and relatives will make you a cup of coffee, change the television channel for you, help tie your shoe laces and so on. They do all these things out of kindness and if the pain is really bad - and you genuinely cannot move - then their help will undoubtedly be received with grateful thanks. But if you allow people to look after you like this all the time then your well-meaning friends and relatives will eventually change your life for you and they will allow you to be dominated completely by your arthritis.

Your friends and relatives will, of course, do these things because they love you, because they don't like to see you suffering and because they feel sympathetic towards you. They don't want to see you struggling and in pain.

But although the sympathy, attention, respect and physical help you get because of your pain and your disease will enable you to avoid work, gardening, household chores (and even sex if you want) your life will be changing and there is a real risk that the change will be permanent.

Gradually, your friends will teach you to behave like an invalid. You will slowly but certainly move away from living a normal life. Because you do not have to make the effort to walk to the corner shop or to pick up your newspaper your joints will stiffen up and eventually you will find that you simply cannot do these things even if you want to.

In the end your friends and relatives will probably feel frustrated as you become more and more of an invalid. They will feel inadequate because, despite all their efforts, your pain and disability will get worse rather than better. They will lose patience. And they won't know what else they can do to help you. They will feel embarrassed and even faintly irritated. And then they will feel guilty. Eventually their visits will become more and more infrequent. By then, however, it will be too late for you to escape from your role as a full time invalid. Because you will have been treated as an invalid and encouraged to think of yourself as an invalid you will have become an invalid. The longer you have been bed or chair bound the more difficult you will find it to break free. Your life will revolve around your pain because you will not be able to do anything else with your life apart from worry about your pain. And, to make things even worse, the weaker and more dispirited you become the more susceptible to pain you will become. You will also probably be addicted to pills of various kinds.

Don't say none of this will happen to you because it can and it will if you let it. Around the world it happens to thousands, probably millions of people, every year.

Learn To Think Positively

There are, however, things that you can do to stop all this happening to you - and to stop yourself being dominated by your pains and your arthritis. The key is that you must try to take a fairly strong and aggressive attitude towards your pain and your illness. You are the only person who can do this. Other people - the people who are closest to you and the professionals who work with you - almost certainly cannot or will not do it for you. Your friends and relatives will be driven by compassion, sympathy and love and their natural response will be to get you to give in to the pain. And the chances are that the professionals looking after you will do the same.

I am not, of course, suggesting that you should try to be a 'hero' and fight your pain or try to ignore it. As I have explained elsewhere that sort of attitude can be dangerous too for you may damage your joints if you try to move them when they are painful and stiff.

But when your pain is less critical you must take the initiative and try to ensure that you - not your arthritis - retain control of your life.

How do you do this?

Well, a good starting point is to try as hard as you can to take an active and positive role in your own treatment. Learn as much as you can about your disease, about what is causing your pain, about what makes it worse and about the ways in which you can help yourself. Reading this book is an excellent starting point for in these pages you will find a considerable amount of information about the various types of arthritis and many practical tips on the best ways to combat the disease.

Ask your doctor to explain things to you when he suggests new pills or other new forms of treatment. Try to regard your arthritis and the pain it brings as an enemy that can be controlled even if it cannot be conquered or banished completely. By doing whatever you can to control your own destiny and by making a genuine effort to take a positive and aggressive role in your own treatment you will help yourself to dominate your disease. By keeping interested and active you will reduce the level of your pain and by remaining positive and aggressive you will strengthen yourself and weaken your arthritis. You should be aware, too, that if you respond to your arthritis in a passive way there will be rewards. You need to be aware of this so that you can resist the temptations that will come your way.

For example, if you stay in bed all day you will be comfortable and warm and because people can see that you are ill they will probably be supportive and sympathetic. If you get out of bed and walk to the shops you may be uncomfortable and the amount of sympathy you receive will probably be less.

This means that getting up and going out and doing things always takes a great deal of determination and courage. To make things easier for yourself try to make sure that you reward yourself as much as you can. When you go out to the shops arrange to meet friends for a coffee or make an extra trip and buy yourself a treat - a book, some music, a new item of clothing.

By treating your pain aggressively and by trying to dominate your arthritis you will ensure that you stay in control of your life. In the end the benefits will be inestimable.

Heat

If you have ever come into the house after a hard day working in the garden or after a long walk in the countryside and sunk yourself into a bathful of warm water then you will know just how soothing and relaxing heat can be. A shower may be an efficient and cheap way of cleaning the body but a warm bath can do things a shower cannot do! Similarly, you have probably felt the relief that a hot water bottle can provide to aching or sore muscles.

Although scientists have studied the subject for years no one is really certain exactly how heat manages to get rid of pain. There are two possible explanations.

First, it may be that heat produces nerve impulses which help to stop pain impulses getting through to the brain (in exactly the same way that rubbing a sore elbow helps to stop the pain messages getting to the brain).

Second, it is known that when the tissues become heated the flow of blood is increased. Some scientists argue that the increased blood flow helps to get rid of chemicals such as histamine and prostaglandins which are responsible for the production of the feeling of pain.

Of course, it doesn't really matter how heat manages to get rid of pain. The important thing is that it does.

Using heat to eradicate pain is not a new phenomenon. In countries all around the world medical historians have shown that doctors have for centuries used hot springs and hot soaking tubs to help patients overcome their pains. It seems that the pains associated with arthritis are especially likely to be controlled or conquered with the aid of heat.

Ice

In a recent research paper an American doctor who specialises in the treatment of pain claimed that after being massaged with ice many of his patients got relief from their pain for up to four hours at a time. The doctor reported that around three quarters of the patients in one group had benefited by using ice. Although the idea of using ice to treat pain may seem a rather odd one many other doctors have experimented with it and have found that ice can sometimes be more effective than heat in the relief of pain!

How on earth can ice help to relieve pain?

One theory is that ice helps to encourage the human body to produce endorphins - special pain relieving hormones. Another is that ice stops pain messages getting through to the brain in much the same sort of way that heat does - by blocking the passage of nerve impulses. And a third theory is that ice closes down the blood vessels and therefore makes the whole area feel numb and anaethetised.

The ice cubes that you get out of your fridge can be used to combat pain but you have to be careful: ordinary ice cubes have sharp edges and can cut! You can get round this problem either by crushing your ice cubes and then wrapping them up in a thin cloth such as a towel or by crushing them and putting them either into a purpose built rubber ice bag or into a hot water bottle. There is no law (yet) that says that a hot water bottle can only be used to keep hot things hot - it can also be used to keep cold things cold! However you wrap your ice you should rub it over the part of your body that is painful. Press fairly firmly and rub the ice either in a backwards and forwards movement or in continuous circles. When you first start rubbing ice on your skin you should feel the cold. Do take care not to hold the ice against your skin for too long because ice - like heat - can burn your skin, and make sure that you keep the ice moving. The moment that your skin starts to feel numb remove the ice and start to move the area.

The Vibrator

Stroking and rubbing a sore area helps to control pain by stimulating the production of sensory nerve impulses which travel quickly along the larger nerve fibres, get to the gate in the spinal cord first and block the passageway of pain impulses. This is how the TENS machine works. If you cannot afford a TENS device, or don't want to buy one, then you may be able to obtain a very similar effect by using a vibrator - exactly the same sort of hand held vibrator as is sold in pharmacies and sex shops for 'personal massage'.

Talk to your doctor and ask him if he thinks your pain could be helped in this way.

Music

Many pain sufferers claim that they obtain relief by listening to music.Some say that they find classical music relaxing. Opera seems popular as a pain reliever. And others say that rock and roll music is most effective for them. A third group enjoy special relaxation tapes - sometimes described as 'new age' music. You can either listen to your music through ordinary speakers or through headphones. Using headphones will enable you to listen to your music without disturbing other people. Some pain sufferers claim that they get a better result by using headphones because they can 'lose' themselves in their music more readily. Music can be soothing and relaxing, cheering and calming.

If you are to get the best out of music then you will have to experiment to find the type of music that helps you most.

Incidentally, do not forget that many pain sufferers get relief by playing their own music. The piano is probably the favourite instrument among those who like to 'lose' their pain in their favourite music.

Your Imagination

The amount of pain that you suffer will depend to a very large extent upon your moods and the frame of your mind. If you are feeling low and bored then you will be far more likely to notice your pain than if you are feeling cheerful and deeply involved in something. But it isn't only the real world which affects the amount of pain you feel. Your imagination can make your pain far more noticeable - and far more destructive. But it can also help you to conquer your pain. If you make an effort to use your imagination to help you then you will almost certainly benefit. For example, in one experiment patients were asked to concentrate on the parts of their bodies where their pains were strongest. They were then asked to imagine that their pain had a 'shape' and had a red line drawn all around it. Next, they were told to imagine that their pain area was getting slowly smaller and smaller. Amazingly, the patients reported that as their imagined pain areas shrank so did the amount of pain they were feeling!

Keep Busy

Many arthritis sufferers try to rest as much as they can. They are reluctant to get too involved in work or in any social activities, partly because of their pain and partly because they don't want to let other people down. Although this is understandable it can be a mistake. Of course, it is vitally important to rest when pain is bad. But resting too much can be bad for you in the long term. Too much inactivity can lead to muscles becoming weak and to essential organs deteriorating. And if you are inactive then the chances are high that you will become bored -

and people who are bored are far more susceptible to pain. So, try to do as much as you comfortably can!

If your work does not provide you with the intellectual stimulation that you need then try attending an evening class at a local college. Or expand your personal library and your regular reading habits. A good book can help you forget your pain as well as a bottle of pills!

How To Sleep - Despite The Pain

It is during sleep that we recharge our physical and mental batteries. Getting a good night's sleep is essential for all of us - and especially vital for anyone who is trying to fight a disease which is as disabling and as exhausting as arthritis. But if you suffer a great deal from arthritis and from pain caused by your arthritis then it is almost inevitable that you will have some difficulty in getting to sleep at night.

Ironically, anyone who suffers from a chronic or persistent pain will confirm that the pain seems to get worse as the day goes on - reaching its worst point fairly late in the evening. And now even the experts have confirmed that this is what happens. Anaesthetists have confirmed that people who suffer from long term pain seem to get the worst pain at around ten o'clock in the evening - just when most folk are getting ready to go to bed. Just to make things worse anxiety and depression and other symptoms also tend to get much worse at this sort of time too.

It is almost as though the arthritis knows that we humans are at our must vulnerable then and so it tries to take advantage of our vulnerability. So, because getting a good night's sleep is so important here are some tips that should help you if your pain keeps you awake.

1. If you find that pain makes sleeping at night difficult or even impossible try taking a nap in the afternoon to 'top up' your sleep requirements. Or trying going to bed earlier in the evening

(before the pain gets really bad). But if you do this do not expect to be able to sleep all through the night as well. I once saw a very indignant patient who complained that he kept waking up at six o'clock every morning. When I talked to him I found that he was going to bed at nine o'clock at night! I had to explain to him that nine hours sleep was really quite enough for anyone. Another patient of mine complained that she couldn't sleep as much as she used to and then confessed that she had a four hour nap every afternoon. Incidentally, the amount of sleep any individual needs varies from time to time and circumstances to circumstances. But very few of us need more than eight hours sleep in any one twenty four hour period. And remember, too, that our need for sleep tends to diminish as we get older. An average sixty year old will probably need no more than six or seven hours sleep a night.

2. Try to make sure that you do not get woken up unnecessarily once you have managed to get to sleep. There are few things more annoying than having to struggle to overcome pain in order to get to sleep and then having to get out of bed an hour later to go to the lavatory. Avoid alcohol, tea, coffee and all other drinks during the evening (alcohol, coffee and tea are all stimulants and are particularly likely to keep you awake). It is also a good idea to make sure that you empty your bladder before you go to bed. If you smoke then do not smoke for at least an hour or two before you go to bed (and certainly don't smoke in bed). Nicotine can have a stimulating effect which will help to keep you awake. Make sure that you don't get woken up because you feel too cold, too hot or too uncomfortable in any other way. If your bedroom is noisy, for example, it might be worthwhile investing in some soundproofing (though bookshelves filled with books make an even better soundproofing system) or double glazing on your windows. Alternatively, buy and use simple ear plugs which can be very effective at keeping out noise.

3. Do make sure that your bed is comfortable. Many people

struggle to get to sleep on a bed that is too soft or too hard. If you suffer from bad joints it is especially important that you make sure that your bed is just right for you. Test a new bed before buying one and if you and your partner need beds with a different amount of spring in them you should be able to find something suitable for beds are now made to cope with this sort of problem. By and large most people with bad joints seem to find a rather firm bed and supportive bed far more comfortable than one which has become very saggy and has no springs left in it.

4. As an arthritis sufferer you will probably be especially susceptible to the cold. And if you are cold when you try to get to sleep at night you will almost certainly fail. So make sure that you are warm! Use a warm duvet (perhaps a warmer one in winter than you use in the summer) because it will be far easier to make the bed afterwards than if you use old-fashioned sheets and blankets. And use an electric blanket or hot water bottle to warm your bed before you get into it (though do make sure that you follow all the precautions - do not sleep in a bed when your electric blanket is switched on, do not use a hot water bottle that is perished or has a loose fitting stopper, do make sure that your hot water bottle is wrapped in a towel or a pillow case and never, ever use an electric blanket and a hot water bottle at the same time). Incidentally, some arthritis sufferers find that they get a lot of relief - and go to bed physically relaxed and more supple - if they have a warm bath before retiring. A shower may save water and may be convenient in many ways but a warm bath can be much better in other ways!

5. I don't think that sleeping tablets are ever likely to be of any real value to people who cannot sleep because of the pain of arthritis. Although I know that millions of people do use sleeping tablets regularly I think there are dangers in doing this - and very few advantages.

CHAPTER SIX:
THE IMPORTANCE OF DIET

Introduction

Numerous claims have made about the importance of diet to arthritis sufferers. I believe that there are only two important dietary factors which influence arthritis (though there are some special dietary restrictions associated with gout).

First, you will be more likely to suffer from arthritis - and more likely to suffer from it badly - if you are overweight. If you carry too much weight then your joints will be constantly under unnecessary pressure. This is particularly true of your weight bearing joints - hips, knees, ankles and spine. The more excess fat you carry the worse the problem will be. Losing weight, and staying slim, is essential if you are to protect your joints.

Second, you will also reduce the risk of developing arthritis if you eat a vegetarian diet and avoid meat completely. A vegetarian diet will also help to control and minimise your symptoms if you are an arthritis sufferer. Recent research done showed that patients with rheumatoid arthritis who followed a vegetarian diet enjoyed a significant reduction in the amount of pain they suffered, in the number of tender and swollen joints they had and in the amount of stiffness they had to endure in the morning. Blood tests also showed that the disease had been brought under better control by the vegetarian diet.

Most of us are brought up to regard meat as the central part of any main meal and as a result we feel slightly 'lost' and uncomfortable when we try to think of a week's menus that don't include any meat. If you don't spend a little time preparing yourself for vegetarianism you will probably end up eating a constant diet of cheese sandwiches and cheese omelettes. If you do this then you will probably make yourself ill. Most cheeses contain quite a lot of fat and you could easily end up eating more fat than you were doing when you were eating meat.

Ten Questions About Becoming A Vegetarian - and The Answers!

Question 1
Is a vegetarian diet safe? I always thought that meat was essential for good health. Won't I be short of essential vitamins and minerals if I stop eating meat?
Answer 1
A vegetarian diet will provide you with all the essential nutrients that your body needs.
Question 2
But what about iron? I thought that iron was only available in meat. And surely iron is essential for the production of healthy blood cells.
Answer 2
Iron is essential for the production of healthy blood cells. But you don't need to eat meat to get a good intake of iron. Dark green vegetables such as cabbage, spinach and kale, peas and beans and dried fruit are among the vegetarian foods which are rich in iron. Moreover, a vegetarian diet will probably increase your body's capacity to absorb iron. Vitamin C - present in large quantities in fruit and vegetables - will help you to absorb iron. Ironically, meat eaters are often more likely to develop iron deficiency anaemia than are vegetarians.
Question 3
Won't a vegetarian diet be short on essential proteins? I thought that there were some types of protein that were only available in meat.
Answer 3
It is true that most of us get the majority of our protein from

meat but that is purely as a result of eating habits rather than anything else. Animal products are, pound for pound, only a very slightly better source of protein than nuts or seeds and no better than things like soya beans. You can get all the protein you need from a vegetarian diet.

Question 4

If I stop eating meat won't I become weak and easily tired?

Answer 4

No. Some of the world's strongest animals - elephants, gorillas, bulls and horses - are vegetarian. Vegetarians have won Olympic medals in strength and endurance events and triathlon championships are regularly won by vegetarians.

Question 5

Apart from helping my arthritis will becoming a vegetarian have any other good effects on my health?

Answer 5

Almost certainly. A vegetarian diet will almost certainly include less fat than a diet that includes meat (unless you eat too many dairy foods). You will, therefore, be less likely to suffer from a wide range of disorders known to be associated with a high fat consumption. Atherosclerosis (clogged up arteries), heart disease and high blood pressure are all associated with a high fat diet. Doctors now estimate that between one third and one half of all cancers are associated with the food we eat and meat and fat are believed to be two of the types of food which can cause cancer. In addition there is now evidence to show that many other disorders are made worse by a diet that includes meat - and better by a vegetarian diet. If you suffer from constipation, for example, you will probably find that eating more fresh fruit and vegetables (and therefore more fibre) will solve your problem permanently. It is also worth remembering that as a non meat eater you will be far less likely to suffer from food poisoning - over 90% of food poisoning cases are due to infected meat.

Question 6

Will a vegetarian diet help me to lose weight?

Answer 6

Yes, you should be able to lose weight more readily if you switch to a vegetarian diet. This will not be because meat is fattening but because by changing your eating habits you will have a chance to get rid of all the old, bad habits that helped to make you fat and to replace them with better, new habits that will help you get slim and stay slim. When you become a vegetarian you can change the way you think about food and you can more easily get into the healthy, new habit of eating only when you are hungry.

Question 7

Will a vegetarian diet be more expensive than an ordinary diet that includes meat?

Answer 7

No. On the contrary a vegetarian diet will probably be cheaper than a diet that includes meat. Meat (and meat products) are expensive to buy. And whereas you can grow some (or all) of your own vegetables you will probably be unable to be able to grow your own meat.

Question 8

Won't I find a vegetarian diet extremely boring? I don't think I could live on a diet of lettuce and cabbage.

Answer 8

I don't think anyone could live on a diet of lettuce and cabbage. But if you think of a vegetarian diet as being inevitably dull that must be because you have been brought up to think of meat as an essential centre-point to every meal. The truth is, however, that vegetables, fruits, pulses and cereals can make an attractive and exciting diet. These days more and more top rank cooks are writing cookery books devoted exclusively to vegetarian recipes.

Question 9

Won't I find it difficult to eat out if I become a vegetarian?

What will I do when I'm travelling or away on holiday?

Answer 9

If you are booking an airline ticket or a hotel simply tell the booking clerk that you are vegetarian. If you are booking a table at a restaurant make sure that they serve vegetarian food. You will have some excellent meals, some quite good meals and some appalling meals. But the rise in popularity of vegetarianism means that it is getting easier and easier to eat out without eating meat. It is usually quite easy to have an excellent vegetarian meal in an Indian restaurant.

Question 10

What can i eat if I don't eat meat?

Answer 10

Many people are put off becoming vegetarian because they can't think what they will be able to eat if they don't eat meat. A quick trip to your local supermarket will, however, show that there are not only many different fruits and vegetables available but that because vegetarianism is growing rapidly there are many ready made vegetarian meals on sale. You will also find many 'meat substitute' meals available. You can buy vegetarian sausages and hamburgers and 'stews' and 'curries' made with soya have the same texture as meals made with meat.

CHAPTER SEVEN:
REST OR EXERCISE?

Introduction

As an arthritis sufferer it is vital that you know when to rest and when to exercise. Too much exercise can cause pain and damage your joints. But too little exercise can lead to your joints becoming stiff and unusable - and can, in the long run, create more pain. When your joints are inflamed they must be rested - and your whole body may need to be rested if you suffer from an inflammatory or auto immune disorder - but if you rest too much your joints will get stuck in one position and your muscles will waste away. It is important, therefore, that you establish a regular, daily exercise programme designed to keep you as supple and as strong as possible. It is much better to do a small amount of exercise every day then a huge amount of exercise once a week.

Important: before beginning any exercise programme you should always consult your own family doctor.

Exercise Rules For Rheumatoid Arthritis

1. Rest is important for sufferers of this disease. If your joints are swollen, stiff and painful then you must rest completely - ideally in bed.

2. Try to use affected joints for short periods of time only. It is important to try to exercise a joint when it is not painful so that you can keep it mobile and prevent it from becoming stiff and unusable.

Exercise Rules For Osteoarthritis

1. General rest is not normally necessary since osteoarthritis usually affects individual joints - but any joint which is painful should be rested.
2. Stiffness can set in if a joint is allowed to 'set' in the same position for more than an hour or so. You should, therefore, put all your affected joints through the full range of possible movements every hour at least. Exercise your joints before going to bed at night - and again, first thing in the morning.
3. You should never exercise when your joints are painful but you should try to exercise as much as you can when they are not painful.
4. If, after exercise, an affected joint aches more than usual - and the ache lasts for two hours or more - then your exercise programme is too severe and needs to be reviewed and downgraded.

Exercise Rules For Ankylosing Spondylitis

1. Mobility rather than rest is the key to the treatment of ankylosing spondylitis. It is important that you try to keep your joints moving. If you allow your joints to rest too much there is a risk that they will seize up completely. But don't exercise if it causes pain - talk to your doctor.

Protect Your Joints Whenever You Can

Even though you need to exercise your joints regularly - and you should try to carry on your life as normally as possible - you must take care not to put too much of a strain on any joint in your body. Here are some tips designed to help you protect your joints from unnecessary stresses and strains:
1. Make sure that your clothes are easy to get into and out of.

Don't have buttons in inaccessible positions. Choose clothes that are roomy rather than constricting.

2. Adjust the height of your bed and of any chairs you use regularly so that you do not have to strain your back, hips or knees when getting in or out of them.

3. Plan your day so that you don't have to go up and down stairs unnecessarily.

4. Never wear shoes that are painful or that do not provide you with sufficient support. Avoid high heeled shoes and make sure that your shoes are big enough. Try to wear shoes that are lightweight rather than heavy boots.

5. Use a shoulder bag rather than a bag that you have to carry in your hand. But don't overfill it with heavy items. And do switch it from shoulder to shoulder.

6. If you have to do a lot of physical work allow yourself enough time to take regular breaks.

7. Try to avoid physical activities which mean putting repeated stress on one particular joint.

8. Do not be shy about using aids and appliances to reduce the strain on your joints

9. Learn how to lift properly in order to reduce the strain on your back, hips and knees.

10. Protect the small joints in your hands by using two hands instead of one whenever possible. And use the palm of your hand and the muscles in your forearm when you need to do any heavy work with your hands - rather than putting all the strain on your fingers (for example, when turning a stiff tap or taking the top off a jar).

How To Lift Without Putting A Strain On Your Joints

Lifting - or trying to lift - heavy objects is a major cause of trouble in the joints of your spine, hips and knees. Follow these tips to help protect your joints.

1. There is no acceptable definition of heavy. Any load can damage your joints if you lift in the wrong way. Always lift carefully and always think before lifting.

2. Whenever possible work out a way to minimise the effort required. If there is a mechanical hoist available - use it. If you can use a trolley or barrow then use one. Unload cupboards and take heavy furniture apart whenever possible. If there is nothing on the object to hold onto then use a sling or put a strong rope underneath it. If there is help available then wait until it arrives. Plan to lift and move heavy objects in gentle, easy stages. Stop if you feel tired - that is when accidents happen.

3. If you have to move a heavy weight on a trolley remember that pulling usually puts less strain on your body than pushing.

4. Make sure that you wear shoes with non slip soles. Do not try lifting or carrying heavy weights while wearing high heels. If possible wear shoes that provide proper protection in case something heavy drops on your feet. And make sure that you use gloves that provide a good grip. Don't try lifting in unusually loose or unusually tight clothing, in clothing that restricts your movements in any way or in clothing that might 'catch' on a protrusion.

5. Stand close to the object you want to lift with your feet apart to improve your balance. Put one foot slightly ahead of the other.

6. Bend your hips and your knees and keep your back straight and your shoulders level and in line with your pelvis. Pick up the object you are lifting with the whole of your hand (rather than just your finger tips) and keep your arms close in to your body. A weight held out at arms' length puts ten times the strain on your spine as a weight held close to your body.

7. Brace your abdominal muscles and then lift the object by straightening your knees. If you are trying to lift something very heavy halve the stress by lifting one end first.If you have to turn move your feet as well as your body and make sure that you do not twist or bend your body while lifting.

8. Try to lift smoothly. And remember to keep the object close

to your body all the time that you are holding it.

9. If the object is too heavy for you put it down straight away.

10. When putting a load down lower yourself by bending your knees and squatting. Do not bend your back when putting something down - this is when injuries often happen.

The Importance Of General Exercise

A good, general exercise programme won't stop you getting pains but it certainly could help strengthen your general level of fitness, increase your resistance to muscular stresses and strains and reduce your susceptibility to joint problems. If you are unfit taking up exercise could be dangerous. If you suddenly throw yourself into a hectic exercise programme you could seriously injure yourself. But not doing any exercise is even worse. Unless you exercise regularly your health will be at risk and in addition to getting backache and arthritis you will be more prone to disorders as varied as osteoporosis, heart disease and depression.

Most of us live fairly sedentary lives. We travel in motor cars, buses and trains and we use gadgets and machines to help us cut down the workload in the house and garden. But your body needs exercise.In a few thousand years time we may well have adapted to our sedentary existence. But at the moment your body is still designed for action. Many of the diseases which are commonest today are partly caused by the fact that most of us do not exercise enough.

So, how much exercise should you do and what should you do?

The first thing you must do is check with your doctor. Don't just rush down to your gym and start lifting the heaviest weights you can find or pedalling the exercise bicycle as fast as it will go - you'll almost certainly make yourself ill if you do. And you could kill yourself. Try to find a gym with a good coach, a well run aerobics class or a sports club that you can join. A good coach is vital: he or she will show you how to take your pulse before and after every exercise session. Within a few weeks you should notice that your pulse will go back to its normal rate quicker and quicker after exercising. You should also notice that your normal pulse rate gets lower as you get fitter.

One of the by-products of taking up an exercise programme is that you'll meet new friends with whom you can share the trials and tribulations of getting fit. You'll do better and get more out of your exercise programme if it is fun so try to choose a type of exercise that you think you'll enjoy.

Allocate time for exercise and stick to it. If you decide to exercise only when you've got a free moment you'll never do anything. You need to set aside time for a properly organised exercise programme. But it need not be much. Three sessions a week will be plenty. You should allow a full hour for each session though to start with you probably won't be able to manage that much. If you are really pushed for time you can squeeze a useful exercise programme into just three twenty minute sessions. Can there be anyone who is so busy that they can't manage one hour a week? Try to make your exercise time inviolable and give it priority over other, less vital tasks.

You don't need a lot of money to take up exercise but do buy the right gear - the best you can afford. Remember: you're not trying to look fashionable but you do need shoes that are comfortable and give good support and since you'll be sweating a lot when you start exercising properly you'll need clothes that can be washed often, quickly and easily.

Finally, remember the most important rule for exercise: it should never hurt. Pain is your body's way of saying stop. If you ignore a pain - and attempt to blunder bravely through the pain barrier - you will almost certainly injure yourself.

General Warnings

1. Do not start an exercise programme until you have checked

with your doctor that the programme is suitable for you. Make sure that you tell him about any treatment you are already receiving and about any symptoms from which you suffer.

2. You must stop exercising if you feel faint, dizzy, breathless or nauseated or if you notice any pain or if you feel unwell in any way. Get expert help immediately and do not start exercising again until you have been given the 'all clear' by your doctor.

Joint Warning: The Wrong Sort Of Exercise Can Damage Your Joints

Your joints can be put under a tremendous amount of strain by any repetitive exercise. As a result arthritis - particularly osteoarthritis in which the joints are 'worn out'- and backache are common problems among sportsmen and athletes who do not take care. Warming up beforehand, resting or even stopping when you feel tired and cooling down gently after an exercise programme are all important.

Running is one of the sports most commonly associated with back, hip and knee injuries. Running tends to tighten the lower muscles of the back causing low back pain and increasing the risk of conditions such as ruptured disc or spondylolysis and runners who exercise for too long on hard surfaces are particularly likely to suffer from backache. Every one hour's running means that your joints get 10,000 vibrations. Running on cambered roads means that the strains on the back are particularly bad because one leg is always running lower than the other.

But running is not, of course, the only sport that can cause joint problems. Virtually any sport can cause trouble. Over enthusiastic swinging of a golf club, for example, can cause nasty strains that may take a long time to heal. The most severe and potentially serious joint injuries tend to occur in contact sports such as rugby and football where a sudden jolt can cause severe damage to almost any joint.

Swimming Is Good For You

Swimming will provide your body will an almost perfect exercise programme. It will improve the efficiency of your heart, it will help improve your muscle strength and it will improve your general flexibility. Swimming is one of the very few types of exercise that helps in these three important different ways.

Swimming will be particularly good for you if you have back or joint trouble because it will enable you to exercise without putting any stress or strain on your joints. The water will support the weight of your body and so you can exercise with the minimum of risk.

The best and most effective strokes are the front and back crawl which will give your whole body a good, general work out. If you swim breast stroke wear goggles and try to learn to swim without keeping your head lifting out of the water all the time. Extending your neck to keep your head out of the water can put a strain on your neck.

Walk Your Way To Health

You don't have to get hot and sweaty to improve your fitness. A gentle walk can help! A study of golfers showed that just walking round a golf course three times a week is enough to reduce the amount of cholesterol in the blood stream and to help get rid of excess weight! And the more you enjoy your game - and the better you are able to forget your worries and anxieties - the more you will benefit from it.

To really benefit from your exercise walk as briskly as you can. Brisk walking can protect your heart just as well as more energetic exercise such as jogging or playing tennis.

You Don't Need To Suffer Pain To Benefit From Exercise!

It is a myth that you need to experience pain to benefit from exercise. Pain is your body's way of saying stop. If you ignore a pain - or try to exercise through it - you will do yourself harm.

Join A Gym!

It is perfectly possible to get all the exercise you need without ever going anywhere near a gym. But if there is a local gym I suggest that you join it! You'll benefit in several ways.

   1. They are bound to have a wider range of equipment than you can buy for yourself.

   2. Good gyms are staffed with well qualified instructors who can help you develop an exercise programme to suit your own personal needs.

   3. You'll find that most gyms are friendly places. You will benefit enormously from the support and companionship of those around you. It is much more fun to exercise in a group than it is to exercise alone.

CHAPTER EIGHT:
ALTERNATIVE SOLUTIONS

Introduction

Here are some simple, introductory guidelines designed to help make sure that you get the best and most appropriate alternative treatment.

1. Orthodox, old-fashioned doctors are, I believe, still best at dealing with emergencies. (And the great majority of the alternative specialists I have spoken to agree with this). Doctors have access to diagnostic equipment (such as X ray machines) and to treatment facilities which are particularly useful when dealing with a patient who has an acute and life threatening problem.

2. Alternative or complementary practitioners seem to be at their best when dealing with chronic or long term problems - and arthritis is one of the diseases they seem best able to help with.

3. In many countries there are still very few regulations governing who can or cannot become an alternative practitioner. Those practitioners who set up in business without being properly trained have done a considerable amount of damage to the image of 'alternative' or 'complementary' medicine. To make sure that you visit someone who is reliable I suggest that you ask around your friends first to see if they know of anyone whom they can recommend. Or ask your own doctor. Most doctors these days know of (and approve of) many alternative medicine practitioners. And it is a myth that your doctor is likely to be cross with you if you tell him that you are planning to visit a complementary practitioner. It is not, I am afraid, safe to rely on the fact that a practitioner you are intending to visit has a list of qualifications after his name. Some of these apparently impressive qualifications can be 'bought' with very little aca-

demic effort. (My cat was once the proud owner of a huge sheaf of diplomas and paper qualifications in alternative medicine).

4. It is important to make sure that you visit a well qualified and well trained practitioner because, contrary to common belief, it is possible for alternative medicines to do harm. Patients who have visited acupuncturists using dirty needles have contracted all sorts of very nasty (and potentially lethal) disorders. Patients who have been given contaminated herbal medicines have been made very ill. There are, I am afraid, risks with alternative medicine just as much as there are risks with orthodox medicine.

5. The best alternative practitioners usually practise from good, clean, well equipped premises. And many good alternative practitioners these days practise in small groups. Personally, I would be wary of anyone who claims to be an expert in a whole range of alternative therapies. Since the training periods for subjects like acupuncture tend to be long and arduous the very best practitioners probably specialise.

Acupuncture

Although acupuncture was first made popular in Europe by a Dutch physician called Willem ten Rhyne it has been used in China for over four thousand years. Rhyne introduced acupuncture to Holland in 1683 but since then it has been regularly rediscovered by traditional Western doctors. Some countries, such as France, have recognised the importance of acupuncture and have special acupuncture departments in many of their major hospitals. In other countries, acupuncture is regarded by many traditional doctors as a 'quack remedy' that should not be taken seriously.

Acupuncture is based upon a theory which says that the human body contains twelve meridians or channels and that it is along these channels that vital, internal energies flow. When these meridians are blocked in some way, goes the theory, the flow of energy will be impeded. And it is this slowing or stopping of the flow of energy which causes illness or pain, say the acupuncturists. The practice of acupuncture is based upon the idea that there are a number of quite specific points on the human body which can be regarded as entry points to this internal energy force. Way back in the fourteenth century Chinese doctors had identified a total of 657 acupuncture points. Since then many other experts have been busy and today experts recognise a total of over 1,000 acupuncture points.

The acupuncturist uses slender needles to clear the blocked meridians and release the flow of energy. The needles can be made of a variety of metals such as silver, gold or copper.

Before starting treatment the acupuncturist makes a diagnosis about the likely cause of the pain (the traditional acupuncture methods of diagnosis involve talking and listening to the patient and then identifying no less than twelve different pulses).

Once he has made a diagnosis the acupuncturist inserts his needles and then manipulates them one by one. He can use several different techniques for manipulating the needles.

* He can insert the needle and twist it backwards and forwards rather vigorously for a few seconds.

* He can put one or more needles into the skin and leave it or them in place for twenty or thirty minutes.

* He can connect the acupuncture needles to an electrical apparatus which passes a mild electric current through them.

* He can dry and shred leaves of the Chinese wormwood plant and then burn these shredded leaves directly over an acupuncture point (this technique is known as moxibustion).

* He can search out tender trigger points and then insert his needles directly into those specific areas.

Despite the scepticism of the traditional medical profession there is no longer any real doubt that this technique does work. Many research papers have been published detailing the value and effectiveness of acupuncture. For example, around twenty years ago four American surgeons reported that they had used acupuncture to treat over three hundred patients in and around the New York area. The surgeons stated that in over three quarters of the cases they had found that acupuncture is one of the most effective treatments available for skeletomuscular disorders such as arthritis. Two doctors writing in an anaesthetics journal in the same year said that 'reports of a large number of surgical cases operated on under acupuncture anaesthesia, with a success rate of up to ninety per cent have now been sufficiently substantiated that the effectiveness of acupuncture can no longer be doubted'.

There is no doubt in my mind that if acupuncture had been a new 'drug' being sold by one of the world's largest and most powerful drug companies it would have been quickly adopted by the world's traditional medical profession. Sadly, however, acupuncture has still not found favour with traditional doctors, some of whom regard it with suspicion because it is not something they were taught about when they were medical students, and some of whom regard it with apprehension because it is a subject they know little or nothing about. There is, I am afraid, a powerful lobby in the medical profession which fights against 'alternative' remedies and which regards treatments such as acupuncture as a serious professional threat. Many doctors fear that if they acknowledge the effectiveness of acupuncture they may lose patients - and fees - to professional acupuncturists.

Back in 1979 acupuncture had been so widely and thoroughly tested that at a meeting of medical representatives from all six of the World Health Organization's regions it was concluded that 'the sheer weight of evidence demands that it must be taken seriously as a clinical procedure of considerable value.'

Today, the consensus seems to be that acupuncture is probably a powerful and effective way of dealing with at least 70% of all long term cases of pain. And, as I have already pointed out, acupuncture is believed to be particularly effective in the treatment of arthritis.

For many years there was some confusion about how acupuncture works but today there are a number of acceptable theories. It seems, for example, that at least two things happen when a needle is pushed into the skin. First, by introducing a sensation into the skin which passes along the larger nerve fibres and closes the gate in the spinal cord, acupuncture prevents pain signals from reaching the brain. And second, when the acupuncture needles are pushed into the skin they also stimulate the production of endorphins (which are the human body's own pain relieving hormones). Some scientists now claim that it is not necessary to follow the traditional acupuncture meridians in order to obtain a useful effect. It is, they say, possible to obtain the same effect by stimulating virtually any point on a fairly large area of skin. In the past it was often claimed that if acupuncture didn't work it was because the acupuncturist had failed to 'hit' the correct acupuncture point. Today, it appears that it may just be that the patient was not one of those who could be helped by acupuncture.

The most dramatic development in the use of acupuncture was probably the fairly recent discovery that it is possible to obtain a type of acupuncture effect without sticking any needles into the skin at all. It is, it seems, perfectly possible to close the spinal cord gate and simulate the production of the vital endorphin hormones simply by applying heat or electrical stimulation to the body, or even by applying simple finger pressure to tender pressure points (this technique, which is not a new one, is usually known as shiatsu or acupressure and is becoming steadily more popular).

Acupressure

Some historians believe that when acupuncture meridians were first mapped out practitioners did not use sharp needles but

used their fingers instead. They argue that the needles so be-
loved of acupuncturists were only introduced to give the therapist the feeling that he was really doing something - and, perhaps, to make the charging of a fee more appropriate.

Acupuncture without needles but with fingers is usually
called acupressure (though a variation of it is called shiatsu)
and as with acupuncture the aim is to restore the flow of energy
along a meridian pathway, stimulating the flow of energy when
there is a blockage and bringing energy into the system when,
for some reason, the meridian is empty.

In order to obtain a useful effect during acupressure the
therapist presses on specific parts of the patient's body, using
only his or her finger tips.

Different therapists seem to use different pressure points
and there does not seem to be a great deal of agreement between different acupressure specialists about the best points to
use in order to treat specific conditions.

The most effective acupressure points seem to be on or
around the head and neck. By using finger massage at the top
of the spine, on the centre of the cheeks, on the outer edges of
the eyes and on the centre of the forehead between the eyes it
is, say the experts, possible to relieve a wide range of symptoms. Another well used acupressure point is the one in the
fleshy web that lies between the thumbs and forefingers of both
hands. Massaging the acupressure point here is said to be particularly useful in the treatment of pain.

Because acupressure is a non invasive, gentle therapy it
is said to be comparatively safe but I would recommend that if
you want to try this form of treatment you consult a well trained
and experienced expert. Acupressure is said to be extremely
useful in the treatment of arthritis pains.

Alexander Technique

The Alexander Technique is built around the idea that the condition and positions of the bones of the spine and the rest of the skeleton have an influence on our health. The Alexander Technique, or Alexander Principle as it is also sometimes known, was first devised nearly a century ago by an actor called F. Matthias Alexander.

Mr Alexander, an Australian, noticed that he kept losing his voice when working on stage and when the medical profession failed to help him he decided to try to investigate and treat his problem himself. He realised that he was losing his voice whenever he was holding his head and neck in a particular position. He surmised that the voice loss was caused by the fact that the position of his neck was squashing his vocal cords.

After experimenting for several months he found that by learning to stand properly, and hold his head up straight, his voice no longer kept on disappearing. So delighted was the actor by this discovery that he retired from the stage and decided to spend his life helping other people conquer their health problems by learning how to stand properly. He believed that just as his voice loss had been caused by poor posture so many other common illnesses might have a similar cause. Alexander's hope was that he would be able to treat problems which had already developed and prevent problems developing in the future, simply by teaching a few basic principles of posture and movement.

And so the Alexander Technique - an educational system designed to help teach people body self awareness, graceful movements and good posture - was created. The aim is to find a patient's bad habits and get rid of them before any real harm is done.

Alexander claimed that people who stand upright and with their heads held high will have their internal organs in the right positions. He argued that such individuals would be far less likely to develop illnesses than individuals who slumped or sat and walked with a poor posture. He claimed that by improving posture and movement patients would be able to improve their digestion, their breathing and their circulation.

Modern followers of F. Matthias Alexander teach patients to move comfortably and to use their bodies properly. The technique is recommended to patients suffering from a wide range of problems but patients with disorders which involve the bones, the joints and the muscles seem particularly likely to benefit.

Individuals who want to benefit from Alexander's discoveries are encouraged to start by looking critically at the way that they sit, stand and walk, as well as the way that they lift and do ordinary, daily jobs around the house. Followers of F.Matthias Alexander claim that every aspect of an individual's life should be examined. They say that even ill fitting shoes can create a whole range of problems. Sore feet can, they say, affect the way that an individual walks and so end up producing serious spine and joint problems.

Homoeopathy

No one really knows how homoeopathy works. But there are thousands of patients who believe that it works. And the risks of side effects developing certainly seem to be slight and today, in an era when doctor-induced illness is commonplace, such an advantage is a fairly major one!

Although homoeopathy can be traced back for centuries, modern homoeopathy was undoubtedly first developed by a man called Samuel Hahnemann, who practised in the early part of the 19th century. Hahnemann was unhappy about the medicines which were available for general medical use at the time. He knew that too many patients were made ill by being given large doses of potentially lethal products and he was, therefore, keen to find a method of treating people that would dramatically reduce the chances of a practitioner doing more harm than good.

Hahnemann knew that both Hippocrates, the father of medicine, and Paracelsus, the man who is widely credited with bringing medicine out of the dark ages and into a scientific era during the Renaissance, had believed that a patient can be cured if he can be given a medicine which will produce symptoms which are the same as the ones produced by his illness. This ancient theory was known as the 'theory of like curing like'.

Although he did not have the ague Hahnemann decided to try to produce the symptoms of the disease in himself. By doing this he was following a long tradition of medical researchers in experimenting upon himself. He knew that cinchona bark, which contains the drug quinine, would relieve the symptoms of the ague and so he took some of the drug to see what happened. He soon developed the symptoms of the disease - including the fever. And when he stopped taking the drug the symptoms disappeared.

Using as his basic principle the theory that 'a substance which produces symptoms in a healthy person will cure those symptoms in a sick person' Hahnemann decided to try to find more substances which would produce the symptoms of disease and during the next few years he experimented with an enormous variety of substances; including animal products, vegetable substances, salts and metals.

By the time he died, in 1843, Samuel Hahnemann had tested and 'proved' the efficacy of 99 different substances and he had created the basis of modern homoeopathy. Even more important he had found that he didn't need to use large substances of the medicines he had 'proved' in order to obtain a useful result. In fact, he found that very small doses made his treatments extremely effective. By the year 1900, just over half a century after his death, over 600 substances had been tested and found to have a useful effect. Today the number of substances available to homoeopaths is around 3,000 and includes honey bee sting venom, snake venom, spiders, gold, copper, sulphur, mercury, onions and Indian hemp! Testings and provings are still continuing in efforts to find more new substances which can be used in homoeopathy.

Making an accurate diagnosis is the first thing a homoeopath must do. He or she will start by asking an enormous number of questions covering mental, physical and emotional issues and designed to help the homoeopath find out as much as possible about the individual. The homocopath will want to know about his patient's personal feelings, needs, anxieties and so on. He will also want to know how his patient responds to outside influences such as the weather and the temperature. In orthodox medicine doctors aim to treat diseases more than patients but in homoeopathy the treatment must be designed to fit the patient.

Having made a diagnosis the homoeopath will then choose a suitable 'medicine' from the list of 3,000. Homoeopaths usually try to find one medicine however many symptoms a patient has. The substance which is finally selected will be given in a very small dose because homoeopaths believe that the smaller the dose the more powerful the response will be. Very small doses are used to trigger a reaction within the body. There are some similarities between homoeopathy and vaccination. In vaccination a small amount of an infective organism is given to the patient to get the body's natural defence mechanisms to start to operate. In homoeopathy a small amount of a drug is given in order to try to stimulate the body's natural defence mechanisms to operate.

The doses which homoeopaths use are so small that they effectively put a drop of concentrated medicine into a bath full of water - and then use a few drops of the bath water as medicine! Homoeopathy does seem to be very safe. But if you want to try this form of alternative medicine you should, of course, consult a properly qualified practitioner.

Osteopathy

Although there undoubtedly are some osteopaths around today who claim that they are able to treat as full a range of diseases as a traditionally trained, allopathic doctor most osteopaths spend most of their time dealing with bone and joint problems. Over half of the patients visiting osteopaths have backache and the majority of osteopaths seem to spend their working lives trying to help patients with back troubles, headaches, neck pains and joint pains of one sort or another.

Some professional osteopaths claim that they are descended (in professional terms) from the very first surgeons and the bonesetters of two hundred years ago. But modern osteopathy was first developed in 1874 by an American called Andrew Taylor Still who was the son of a Methodist preacher. Still, who hated drugs and alcohol, believed that the human body could be treated as a machine. He felt that it was faults in the musculo-skeletal system which were responsible for many diseases.

Most osteopaths make an initial diagnosis by watching the way that their patients walk and stand and sit. They supplement these observations by talking and listening to their patients and by studying X rays. Osteopathic treatment usually involves a mixture of manipulation and massage.

It is vitally important to remember that osteopathy can produce problems and in order to minimise the risks you should only visit a practitioner who has been fully trained and you should make sure that he is well aware of your condition. There are many conditions - fractures, tumours, infection, inflammation and so on - which increase the chances of things going wrong.

Hypnotherapy

The Egyptians were fascinated by hypnotherapy several thousand years ago and then, for quite a long while, this speciality virtually disappeared from view.

In the seventeenth century a man called Athanasius Kircher played around with the idea for a while. It was, however, a man called Franz Mesmer, who worked in the eighteenth century, who really brought hypnosis and hypnotherapy back into vogue. The first evidence that hypnotherapy could help patients who were suffering from pain came from work done in the middle of the eighteenth century by a surgeon called James Esdale. Esdale claimed that he had performed three hundred major surgical operations in India using hypnosis as the only anaesthetic.

During recent years hypnotherapy has come back into fashion again and today there are many people who claim that it is a good way to deal with pain in general and arthritis in particular. Studies have been done which have shown that hypnotherapy can be used to increase both the pain threshold (the point at which pain is felt) and pain tolerance (the amount of pain that an individual can put up with).

Sadly, today there are many hypnotherapists around who have not (to be polite) received a very exhaustive training and there are some professionals who worry that the services offered by these practitioners may prove dangerous. If you think that you would like to try hypnotherapy as a way of combating the pain of your arthritis I would recommend that you talk to your own doctor and ask him to arrange for you to see a professional and fully qualified hypnotherapist.

Healing

The difference between 'healing', 'spiritual healing' and 'faith healing' cause some confusion. Here, however, are definitions which are commonly used:

* healing: the word is used to describe the whole phenomenon of healing with medicines or without any obvious intervention by the healer

* faith healing: the patient trusts the healer and there is a powerful link between the patient's mind and his body

* spiritual healing: the patient may or may not know that

the healing is taking place. He may or may not be receptive. The healer transmits energy from himself to the patient in some way.

Healers work in a variety of different ways. Some healers lay their hands on their patients. Others hold their hands above the patient's body. And there are healers who claim that they can heal someone without seeing him or her or, indeed, being anywhere near him or her. Some healers encourage patients and relatives to take part in the process of healing. Some talk or pray and some are silent. Healing can be used for just about any condition and there is no doubt that many patients with arthritis have benefited from healing. The majority of healers do not charge a fee for their services.

APPENDIX:
AIDS FOR ARTHRITIS SUFFERERS

Because of stiffness in their joints arthritis sufferers often have difficulty in walking, bending or reaching. The damage arthritis can do can be so severe that it can cause disablement -and even crippling. To help overcome these problems there are many commercially available products available. In addition there are many aids and gadgets which make life easier for the arthritis sufferer, which reduce the need for bending, reaching and lifting and which help to protect the joints and prevent the development of problems.

The best aids will help you to make the most of all your remaining skills and will minimise the effect that your disabilities have on your life.

Some arthritic patients are reluctant to use aids at all. They fear that to rely on any sort of assistance is to admit to a weakness; they even fear that it will speed up the disabling process. Nothing could be further from the truth.

The other fear, that gadgets and aids must inevitably cost a lot of money, is also ill founded. There are, it is true, some pieces of equipment (particularly the electrical ones) which cost a lot of money. But there are also gadgets which cost next to nothing and which can be made at home.

This appendix does not attempt to offer a comprehensive list of aids for arthritis sufferers but is designed to show the range of aids available. You should be able to obtain a full list of available aids from your family doctor or hospital consultant but if you have any difficulty I suggest that you contact one of the many charitable or commercial organisations offering aids for the disabled. Big cities often have shops which specialise in offering equipment designed to make life easier for arthritis sufferers.

Aids For Sitting

Posture stool
The seat slopes forwards and you sit with your weight resting on your knees and your feet tucked in underneath you. The posture stool is designed to encourage you to sit in a healthier position so that you can get up at the end of a day's work without having a stiff and aching back.

Backrests, 'wedges' and lumbar supports
Most chairs do not provide enough support for the lumbar part of the spine. You can buy many different supports - including inflatable cushions which are suitable for travellers - which will help turn your uncomfortable chair into one which is much friendlier to your back and other joints.

Adjustable chairs
Properly adjustable chairs which allow you to sit in a comfortable position are available. But they do tend to be expensive. The seat height should be adjustable as should the angle of the seat and the backrest. You'll find it easier to get into and out of chairs which have arm rests that you can rest your weight on when sitting down or push against when standing up. If your feet aren't resting on the floor when you are sitting down then you need a footrest (dangling feet add to the stress on your spine).

Ejector chairs
It is possible to buy chairs which, at the touch of a lever, help to push you up into the standing position.

Aids For Work

Writing slopes
If you work on a computer, word processor or typewriter you

may need to have a flat desk. But writing slopes enable you to work at an angle which is better suited to your body.

Tip for surviving at work
Get up and walk about every half an hour or so. This will give you a chance to stretch your back and will help prevent muscle, joint and ligament strain.

Aids For Picking Things Up

Simple 'pick up sticks' (such as are often used by park attendants employed to pick up bits and pieces of waste paper) help make life much easier if you find it difficult to bend or to reach for small objects. Pick up sticks are probably the most versatile and useful of all gadgets for the arthritic and disabled. They are basically nothing more than a pair of tongs with a long handle which enable you to pick up something without bending or stretching. They are also useful for drawing curtains, switching on lights, pulling on socks and doing a thousand and one other potentially painful little chores. With a little experience you will find that a pick up stick extends your reach by three feet and enables you to pick up all sorts of things (clothes, books, magazines, newspapers, rubbish etc) off the floor without bending down. It is possible to buy sticks which fold up (so that you can carry them around with you) and some sticks have magnets on the end to help pick up metal objects.

Aids In The Kitchen

If you have arthritis in your hands or wrists then you will almost certainly find that one of the most useful aids available is a small device which will help you to open a jar. There are also aids available to help you lift a heavy kettle or open a can (wall mounted can openers are sometimes helpful). Some useful aids can easily be made by anyone with a few basic carpentry skills.

Dealing with or preparing food can be tricky but the patient with only one useful hand will find that a spiked board will enable him to keep vegetables still while they are being peeled and chopped. To open packets it may help to stand them upright in a kitchen drawer, close the drawer as far as it will go and then cut the top of the packet open with a knife. Kitchen tools are easier to get hold of if they are hung neatly on hooks rather than placed inaccessibly in drawers. Cutlery should have large handles and you can adapt cutlery to make it easier to use by using tape or even bicycle handlebar rubbers.

One of the simplest and most useful gadgets you can buy if you have arthritic hands is a 'grip mat' - a small, non stick rubber mat that can be invaluable for opening jars, bottles or even doors that are stuck tight.

If you are planning a new kitchen think carefully about the height at which you have cupboards and electrical sockets placed (it is possible to buy electric plugs fitted with handles - these are much easier to pull out and push in than ordinary household plugs). Try to make sure that everything you need is within easy reach.

Remember that taps are easier to turn on and off if they are of the lever type.

Aids In The Bathroom

If you have arthritis in your hands then you will probably find it difficult to operate ordinary taps so long handled, lever type taps (the sort used by surgeons in operating theatres) can be a tremendous help. Or you can obtain taps which can provide either hot or cold water with the same lever. A liquid soap dispenser which can be operated either by a foot pedal or by a lever will make washing much easier. If holding a nail brush is difficult one can be fixed to the side of the wash basin by screwing suction cups onto the back of the brush and sticking the suckers onto the basin.

As far as the bath is concerned one of the most important aids is probably the bathrail or handrail. A rubber mat in the bottom of the bath will prove useful for anyone who is slightly unsteady. People who find it difficult to lie down may be better off with a seat or board placed firmly across the bath. A lift suspended over the bath may be helpful (all sorts of hoists are available) and there are even special baths available in which the bather sits rather than lies.

There are many other useful gadgets for the bathroom: sponges with long handles, tap turners, long handled brushes, toothbrushes with built up handles and so on. Often it is not necessary to buy an aid for a home made improvisation will prove equally effective. For example, it is possible to make a tap turner with a piece of wood that has a hook fastened onto it. And it is possible to build up the handle of a toothbrush to a more manageable size either by wrapping pieces of sticking plaster over it or by fitting a bicycle handlebar rubber onto the handle.

As with everything else it is best to isolate the problems first and then look for the solutions. The solutions will often appear quite simple. For example, if someone finds it difficult to operate a bathroom pull switch they may find it easier if a ball is tied onto the end. One of those 'air' balls that golfers use for practise will be easy to tie on.

There are things that can also be done to make the other vital piece of bathroom equipment - the lavatory - more accessible. The toilet seat can be raised so that the stiff person does not have so much bending to do. And soft absorbent loose-leaf tissue is easier to handle than a continuous roll - and easier to use too.

Finally, it is always wise to have several grab handles near to the lavatory, which should be very well secured.

Walking Aids

Many arthritic patients are reluctant to use a walking stick. They think of it as a badge of infirmity. It should be thought of as an aid to walking - just as good shoes are an efficient walking aid. There are many different types of stick available -ranging from the ordinary wooden stick (which should have a rubber tipped end to ensure that it does not slip) to the tripod type of stick (which has three feet attached to a single handle and which will stand up by itself - it gives a bit more security than an ordinary stick but is almost as portable).

The walking frame is held in front - usually with both hands. When moving the right side of the frame and the left side are shuffled forwards alternately. The frames are usually made of light but strong material and one major advantage is that a basket can be attached to the front so that small items (books, shopping etc) can be carried around. Some frames can be converted into seats.

When choosing a stick or frame do make sure that it is the right size. Frames usually have adjustable handles. Sticks should be tried out for size. Some collapsible sticks and frames can be obtained.

A stick or frame can give you extra support, take some of the strain and enable you to rest when you need to. If you use a stick change hands regularly so that you don't get into the habit of putting too much strain on one side of your body.

Wheelchairs

There are many different types of wheelchair so when selecting a wheelchair you need to know exactly what you are going to use it for. Wheelchairs can be divided into three main groups: those most suitable for outdoor use, those suitable for use indoors and those which can be used either indoors or out of doors. Decide whether your chair will be pushed or propelled from inside. Look for a chair that is manœuvrable and, ideally, collapsible so that you can take it with you when you travel by car, train or bus. Some chairs have detachable armrests and hinged footrests which make them easier to use because you can get in and out without too much trouble. Propelling wheels (the bigger wheels that the occupant moves to get a chair moving) are usually at the rear but if you have limited shoulder movement you may get on better with a chair which has the propelling wheels at the front. Pneumatic tyres are more comfortable - particularly over rough ground - but solid tyres make a chair easier to move and they do not puncture. If you are going to use your wheelchair over long distances you may get on better with a powered model. There are all sorts of different powered wheelchairs available: some suitable only for indoor use, some suitable for use on quite rough ground. It really is a good idea to shop around - but first, make sure that you know what you want.

Aids For Shopping

If you have to carry heavy loads around use a shopping trolley or basket on wheels to relieve the strain on your back. Recent research from France showed that the average six year old French child regularly carries 9% of his or her body weight in a rucksack or satchel while travelling to and from school. By the age of twelve the load has risen to 25% and by the time they reach sixteen years of age pupils are carrying 50% of their bodyweight around with them in books, sports gear etc. It is hardly surprising that in the last decade the number of French citizens suffering from severe back problems has risen from 30% to 45%.

Aids For Getting Up and Down Stairs

If you find walking up and down stairs painful you may find it easier if you edge yourself up or down stairs on your bottom. If your problem persists investigate the possibility of installing a powered stair lift. You sit down on a small chair, press a button and ascend or descend the stairs effortlessly.

Aids For Getting Dressed

If you have difficulty in bending or raising your arms you will find that some clothes are far more difficult to get into and out of than others. Avoid tight jeans or trousers. Wear slip on shoes rather than lace ups. Make sure that zips and buttons are easily accessible and replace difficult to reach and difficult to use fasteners with easy to reach and easy to use fasteners. Velcro fastenings are easy to close and undo. (Arthritic fingers will find buttons, hooks and eyes and other small fasteners difficult or impossible). Buttons, when you do use them, should be as large as possible. The long-handled shoe horn, the shoe which has an elasticated front and the long handled pick up stick can all help. For women a wrap around skirt is easier to put on than one that has to be pulled up while a front fastening brassiere can be a great help.

Disposable underwear, towels and handkerchiefs may be expensive but do cut down on washing and ironing.

Tips for dressing
* Lean against a wall when you need to raise a foot or leg (eg to put on a sock or tie a shoelace)
* Roll up clothes (eg jumpers) so that you can put your arms through the arm holes as easily as possible
* If you have difficulty in balancing and pulling on trousers or tights try dressing while lying on top of your bed. To get your

trousers over your feet pull your knees up to your chest. Then straighten your legs to pull your trousers up to your bottom.

Getting about

If you have difficulty in driving an ordinary car look at the possibility of having a car 'customised'. You can buy better car seats and backrests to make sitting in a car more comfortable. Wide angle mirrors make driving safer if you have limited neck movement. There are special knobs available which can be attached to the steering wheel to make steering easier.

Housing: general advice

Many of the minor hazards which the perfectly fit take in their stride can become major problems when joints stiffen and limbs don't work as well as they did.

For example, a flight of stairs which a fit and healthy individual can run up and down without any thought will provide an arthritic patient with considerable problems. Even a single high step or a couple of steps at the front door can suddenly become a restrictive barrier. High rise blocks of flats where lifts may be out of order for months on end can turn into high rise prisons for the disabled. And the lack of a ground floor lavatory can mean a disabled person becoming marooned on the first floor.

Just as important as the type of home is where the accommodation is situated. A bungalow may seem a wonderful idea. But if it is as the top of a steep hill, hidden away in the country miles from a bus stop or railway station, or can only be reached by clambering up a steep path or a long flight of stone steps, it may be completely unsuitable for someone disabled by arthritis.

When planning a new home, or redesigning an existing one, it is important to be aware of the potential hazards and to think of future problems too. Uneven floors, steps between rooms and difficult passageways are all potential troublespots.

Aids for hobbies and leisure

Just because you are arthritic you don't have to give up all your favourite sports and hobbies. There are many gadgets that you can use. If you like playing cards you can make a 'card holder' by sawing a suitably sized slit in a piece of wood. If you like reading but find it difficult to hold a book then put a tray with a small stand on your lap. If you like sewing but have difficulty in threading a needle then buy a self threading needle or an automatic threading machine. For the arthritic gardener there are plenty of useful tools: long handled gadgets for hoeing and weeding and picking up the rubbish, lawn mowers that can be operated from a wheelchair, spades and forks that can be used without bending and tools that can be used with just one hand for cutting long grass and pruning small bushes and trees. There are long handled trowels, kneeler stools for gardeners with dodgy knees and all sorts of gadgets for use in the greenhouse. Finally, gardeners who have a lot of difficulty in bending can try building up their gardens to waist height. Flower and vegetable beds can be separated by firm, even concrete paths. Raised gardens are suitable for arthritics who have to do all their gardening from a wheelchair.

Vernon Coleman 1996

For a catalogue of Vernon Coleman's books
please write to:

Publishing House
Trinity Place
Barnstaple
Devon EX32 9HJ
England

Telephone   01271 328892
Fax   01271 328768

Outside the UK:
Telephone   +44 1271 328892
Fax   +44 1271 328768

Or visit our websites:

www.vernoncoleman.com
www.lookingforapresent.com
www.makeyourselfbetter.net

Other books by Vernon Coleman

How To Overcome Toxic Stress
and the Twenty-First Century Blues

'Never have I read a book that is so startlingly true. I was dumbfounded by your wisdom. You will go down in history as one of the truly great health reformers of our time'
(Extracted from a letter to the author)

If you are frustrated, bored, lonely, angry, sad, tired, listless, frightened, unhappy or tearful then it is possible that you are suffering from Toxic Stress.

After three decades of research Dr Coleman has come up with his own antidote to Toxic Stress which he shares with you in this inspirational book. In order to feel well and happy again you need to take a close look at your life and put things back in the right order. Dr Coleman shows you how to value the worthwhile things in life and give less time to things which matter very little at all. The book contains hundreds of practical tips on how to cope with the stresses and strains of daily life.

Price £9.95 (paperback)

Published by European Medical Journal
Order from Publishing House, Trinity Place, Barnstaple,
Devon EX32 9HJ, England

Other books by Vernon Coleman

The Traditional Home Doctor

Vernon Coleman has been writing about health matters for over 25 years and readers have sent him countless thousands of tips and helpful hints. These tips and hints are the sort of information that isn't going to go out of date; they are good, old-fashioned, tried-and-tested methods that have worked for people over the years.

You will find this book a great help the next time you are faced with a family health problem.

The book contains easy-to-follow tips on:

Allergies	Anorexia
Babies	Backache
Burns	Catarrh
Colds	Flu
Constipation	Cystitis
Hay Fever	High Blood Pressure
Headaches	Indigestion
Stress	Prostate Problems
Sleeplessness	Women's Problems
Tiredness	and much more

Each topic includes tips and hints for solving the problem or reducing troublesome symptoms.

Price £9.95

Published by EMJ Books
Order from Publishing House, Trinity Place, Barnstaple,
Devon EX32 9HJ, England

Other books by Vernon Coleman

Mindpower

Nothing has the potential to influence your health quite as much as your mind. We've all heard the phrase "you'll worry yourself to death" and scientists have now proved that it is indeed possible for your mind to at least make you ill if not actually kill you. Most doctors around the world now agree that at least 75% of all illnesses can be caused or made worse by stress and/or anxiety. But although your mind can make you ill it can also make you better and has an enormous capacity to heal and cure if only your know how to harness its extraordinary powers and make them work for you - instead of against you!

You can use Mindpower to help you deal with a range of problems including: Anxiety, Depression, Arthritis, Cancer, Asthma, Diabetes, Eczema, Headaches, Heart Disease, High Blood Pressure, Indigestion, Women's Problems, Migraine, Pain and Sleeplessness.

"Dr Coleman's Mindpower is based on an inspiring
message of hope."
(Western Morning News)

"... offers an insight into the most powerful healing agent in
the world - the power of the mind."
(Birmingham Post)

Price £9.95

Published by EMJ Books
Order from Publishing House, Trinity Place, Barnstaple,
Devon EX32 9HJ, England

Other books by Vernon Coleman

Food For Thought

Between a third and a half of all cancers may be caused by eating the wrong foods. In this bestselling book Dr Coleman explains which foods to avoid and which to eat to reduce your risk of developing cancer. He also lists foods known to be associated with a wide range of other diseases including Asthma, Gall Bladder Disease, Headaches, Heart Trouble, High Blood Pressure, Indigestion and many more.

Years of research have gone into the writing of this book which explains the facts about mad cow disease, vegetarian eating, microwaves, drinking water, food poisoning, food irradiation and additives. It contains all the information you need about vitamins, carbohydrates, fats and proteins plus a list of 20 superfoods which Dr Coleman believes can improve your health and protect you from a wide range of health problems. The book also includes a "slim-for-life" programme with 48 quick slimming tips to help you lose weight safely and permanently.

" ... a guide to healthy eating which reads like a thriller"
(The Good Book Guide)

"Dr Vernon Coleman is one of our most enlightened, trenchant and sensible dispensers of medical advice"
(The Observer)

Price £9.95

Published by EMJ Books
Order from Publishing House, Trinity Place, Barnstaple,
Devon EX32 9HJ, England

Also available by Vernon Coleman

Superbody

A healthy immune system won't simply protect you against infection - it will also prove to be an essential factor in your body's ability to fight off all other diseases - including cancer.

The first two parts of this book explain why and how our bodies are under siege - and why the incidence of cancer and infectious diseases is rising rapidly (and likely to continue rising).

Infectious diseases started to become resistant to antibiotics a quarter of a century ago. Since then the situation has steadily worsened and it is now probably too late for the medical profession to reverse the situation. Infectious diseases are coming back in a big way and the incidence of cancer is also going to continue to rise.

And so the third part of *Superbody* explains how you can protect yourself against these, and other threats, by improving the strength, efficiency and effectiveness of your immune system.

Price £9.95 (paperback)

Published by European Medical Journal
Order from Publishing House, Trinity Place, Barnstaple,
Devon EX32 9HJ, England

Also available by Vernon Coleman

Around the Wicket

Edward Pettigrew's Diary Of A Year At Little Lampton Cricket Club

All cricket lovers will know that it is almost compulsory for anyone who plays professional cricket to write a diary detailing their adventures on and off the field. Often these literary offerings seem little more that self-congratulatory advertisements designed, on the one hand, to describe in nauseating and extensive detail the cricketer's talent, natural abilities and, on the other, his misfortune at having to play his professional cricket at a time when his county and national side were managed by ruthless incompetents whose sole purpose in life was to find excuses to leave him out of their sides!

In total contrast, Vernon Coleman believes that true cricket, in its purest sense, is played at local level, and so he decided to pen this diary (along with Edward, of course!) as a tribute to the glories and glitches of village and town cricket. And so, although today's professional game might seem to have been taken over by marketing men in smart suits, you can still find real cricket alive and well throughout England. This book follows one traditional village team throughout a year's cricketing activity (on and off the field!).

Price £9.95 (paperback)

Published by Chilton Designs
Order from Publishing House, Trinity Place, Barnstaple,
Devon EX32 9HJ, England

Also available by Vernon Coleman

Bodypower
The secret of self-healing

A new edition of the sensational book which hit the Sunday Times bestseller list and the Bookseller Top Ten Chart. This international bestseller shows you how you can harness your body's amazing powers to help you cure 9 out of 10 illnesses without seeing a doctor!

The book also covers:

- How your personality affects your health
- How to stay slim for life
- How to break bad habits
- How to relax your body and mind
- How to improve your figure
- And much much more!

"Don't miss it. Dr Coleman's theories could
change your life" (Sunday Mirror)

"A marvellously succinct and simple account of how the body
can heal itself without resort to drugs" (The Spectator)

"Could make stress a thing of the past" (Woman's World)

Price £9.95

Published by EMJ Books
Order from Publishing House, Trinity Place, Barnstaple,
Devon EX32 9HJ, England

Also available by Vernon Coleman

People Watching

This fascinating book examines the science and art of people watching. By reading the book and following its advice you will be able to:

- Understand gestures and body language
- Look like a winner
- Negotiate successfully
- Make people like you
- Avoid being manipulated
- Look sexy
- Survive on the street

"The ubiquitous media-doc has done it yet again, this time turning his talents for producing gems of information in rapid-fire sequence to the field of body language and private habits.Once you start to browse you would have to be a hermit not to find it utterly "unputdownable".'
(The Good Book Guide)

"People Watching by Vernon Coleman explains everything you need to know about body language and also how to read individuals by their style of clothes and the colours they wear. There are tips on how to make people like you and how to be a successful interviewee. If you want to look sexy for that special someone or you just want to impress the boss you'll be a winner with this book" (Evening Telegraph)

Price £9.95
Published by Blue Books
Order from Publishing House, Trinity Place, Barnstaple, Devon EX32 9HJ, England

Also available by Vernon Coleman

The Bilbury Chronicles

A young doctor arrives to begin work in the small village of Bilbury. This picturesque hamlet is home to some memorable characters who have many a tale to tell, and Vernon Coleman weaves together a superb story full of humour and anecdotes. The Bilbury books will transport you back to the days of old-fashioned, traditional village life where you never needed to lock your door, and when a helping hand was only ever a moment away. The first novel in the series.

"I am just putting pen to paper to say how very much I enjoyed The Bilbury Chronicles. I just can't wait to read the others."
(Mrs K., Cambs)

"...a real delight from cover to cover. As the first in a series it holds out the promise of entertaining things to come"
(Daily Examiner)

"The Bilbury novels are just what I've been looking for. They are a pleasure to read over and over again"
(Mrs C., Lancs)

Price £12.95 (hardback)

Published by Chilton Designs Publishers
Order from Publishing House, Trinity Place, Barnstaple, Devon EX32 9HJ, England

Also available by Vernon Coleman

Bilbury Grange

The second novel in the Bilbury series sees the now married
doctor moving into his new home - a vast and rambling country
house in desperate need of renovation. With repair bills soaring
and money scarce, the doctor and his new wife look for additional ways to make ends meet. Another super novel in this series - perfect for hours of escapism!

"I have just finished reading Bilbury Grange. I found the book
to be brilliant. I felt as though I was part of the community.
Please keep me informed of any more in this excellent series."
(Mr C, Cleethorpes)

"A wonderful book for relaxing and unwinding. Makes you
want to up roots and move to the rural heartland."
(Lincolnshire Echo)

"For sheer relaxing pleasure here's another witty tale from the
doctor whose prolific writings are so well known."
(Bookshelf)

Price £12.95 (hardback)

Published by Chilton Designs Publishers
Order from Publishing House, Trinity Place, Barnstaple,
Devon EX32 9HJ, England

Also available by Vernon Coleman

The Bilbury Revels

Disaster strikes in this the third Bilbury novel when a vicious storm descends on the village. The ensuing snow storm cuts off the village and blankets the whole area in a deep carpet of snow. Much damage is done to the village as a result of the storm and the locals band together to undertake the repair work. Money, as ever, is tight and fund-raising is of prime importance. Money-spinning suggestions are sought and so the idea of the Revels is born - a week of fun and festivities to raise the money needed to repair the local schoolteacher's cottage.

Price £12.95 (hardback)

Bilbury Pie

A delightful collection of short stories based in and around this fictional Devon village. Every community has its characters and Bilbury is no exception! Thumper Robinson is the local "jack the lad" and Pete is the taxi driver, shop owner, funeral director and postman all rolled into one. Patchy Fogg dispenses advice on antiques to anyone who will listen and Dr Brownlow is the eccentric and rather elderly, retired local doctor.

Price £9.95 (hardback)

Published by Chilton Designs Publishers
Order from Publishing House, Trinity Place, Barnstaple,
Devon EX32 9HJ, England

Also available by Vernon Coleman

Bilbury Country

The fourth book in the Bilbury series set in idyllic Exmoor village. This novel sees the usual peace and tranquillity enjoyed by the locals destroyed by an invading army of tourists.

Does this invasion of holidaymakers mean financial reward for the locals - or will it threaten their much-loved way of life?

All the familiar and colourful characters are here to tell yet another spellbinding tale in this ever-popular series.

Price £12.95 (hardback)

Published by Chilton Designs Publishers
Order from Publishing House, Trinity Place, Barnstaple,
Devon EX32 9HJ, England

Alice's Diary

Well over 16,000 delighted readers from around the world have bought this wonderful book which tells of a year in the life of a mixed tabby cat called Alice.

Alice records the year's events and disasters with great humour and insight and at long last gives us a glimpse of what it is really like to be a cat! Delightfully illustrated throughout, this book is an absolute must for animal and cat lovers everywhere.

Price £9.95 (hardback)
Published by Chilton Designs Publishers
Order from Publishing House, Trinity Place, Barnstaple,
Devon EX32 9HJ, England

Alice's Adventures

After the publication of her first book Alice was inundated with fan mail urging her to put pen to paper once more. The result is this, her second volume of memoirs in which she shares with us another exciting and eventful year.

This delightfully illustrated book is full of the wry and witty observations on life which so delighted the readers of her first book.

Another "must" for cat lovers everywhere.

Price £9.95 (hardback)

Published by Chilton Designs Publishers

Order from Publishing House, Trinity Place, Barnstaple, Devon EX32 9HJ, England

The Man Who Inherited a Golf Course

The title says it all! Trevor Dukinfield, the hero of the story, wakes up one morning to discover that he is the owner of his very own golf club - fairways, bunkers, clubhouse and all. It has been left to him in his uncle's will, but there are some very strange conditions attached to his inheritance. To keep the club he must win an important match. The only snag is that he has never played a round of golf in his life.

Price £12.95 (hardback)

Published by Chilton Designs Publishers
Order from Publishing House, Trinity Place, Barnstaple, Devon EX32 9HJ, England

Deadline

After losing his job on a national newspaper, Mark Watson is approached by a former colleague whose wife has mysteriously disappeared. Despite his total lack of experience, Watson finds himself offering to help locate the missing woman. Before he know it has finds himself embarked on a new career - that of private investigator. You'll be gripped by this thriller set in London and Paris.

Price £9.95 (hardback)

Published by Chilton Designs Publishers
Order from Publishing House, Trinity Place, Barnstaple,
Devon EX32 9HJ, England

Mrs Caldicot's Cabbage War

A truly inspiring novel about a woman who embarks on the adventure of a lifetime following the unexpected death of her husband. Pushed from pillar to post by an uncaring family who are determined to rule her life, she fights back with amazing results. Full of the gentle humour and wonderful storytelling for which Vernon Coleman is so well-loved.

Price £9.95 (hardback)

Published by Chilton Designs Publishers
Order from Publishing House, Trinity Place, Barnstaple,
Devon EX32 9HJ, England

The Village Cricket Tour

This superb novel tells the story of a team of amateur cricketers who spend two weeks of their summer holidays on tour in the West Country. It proves to be a most eventful fortnight full of mishaps and adventures as the cricketers play their way around the picturesque coastline of Devon and Cornwall.

"The only word to describe (this book) is hilarious. It is the funniest book about cricket that I have ever read. In fact it is the funniest book I have read since Threee Men in a Boat. Anyone interested in cricket will find this book irresistable."
(Chronicle & Echo)

Price £12.95 (hardback)

Published by European Medical Journal
Order from Publishing House, Trinity Place, Barnstaple,
Devon EX32 9HJ, England